SUSAN B. ANTHONY

ILENE
COOPER

SUSAN B. ANTHONY

FRANKLIN WATTS
NEW YORK I LONDON I TORONTO I SYDNEY I 1984
AN IMPACT BIOGRAPHY

A GROLIER COMPANY

Cover photograph courtesy of Culver Pictures.

Photographs courtesy of
Culver Pictures: pp. 18, 36, 39, 48, 68, 86;
Sophia Smith Collection (Women's History Archives),
Smith College: pp. 31, 79, 105, 110.

Library of Congress Cataloging in Publication data

Cooper, Ilene.
Susan B. Anthony.

(An Impact biography)
Includes index.
Summary: A biography of one of the first leaders
of the campaign for women's rights who helped
organize the women's suffrage movement.
1. Anthony, Susan B. (Susan Brownell), 1820–1906—
Juvenile literature. 2. Feminists—United States—
Biography—Juvenile literature. [1. Anthony, Susan B.
(Susan Brownell), 1820-1906. 2. Feminists] I. Title.
HQ1413.A55C66 1984 324.6′23′0924 [B] [92] 83-21788
ISBN 0-531-04750-4

CONTENTS

For Robert,
who never failed me

The author would like to thank
Iva Meyers Freedman and Dale Matten
for their assistance.

BERKSHIRE BEGINNINGS

1

Suppose for a moment that you are a young woman living in the United States during the early part of the nineteenth century. You, along with slaves and Indians, cannot vote. It is unlikely that you will work outside the home, but if you do, and you are married, your husband has the right to take all your wages. Likewise, any inheritance that a parent or relative leaves you automatically becomes his property. He can apprentice a child without your consent, and though divorce is rare, should you have one, your husband will receive custody of the children. If you protest any mistreatment by your husband, the courts would consider it unfortunate but they would not intervene.

You would have slightly more freedom but much less status if you remain unmarried. Spinsters, derogatorily nicknamed "old maids," are scorned and pitied for not fulfilling a woman's natural function of taking care of a husband and children. As a single woman you are expected to remain under your father's roof; after his death a relative, sometimes willingly, often not, will take you in. Because you have little education, there is almost no opportunity for work. If you have to support yourself you will be either a domestic, a seamstress, or a teacher depending on your station in life. Money or property left you will probably be administered by a male guardian who can dispense it at his whim.

The struggle for women's rights continues today. Yet, much has been accomplished during the last 150 years or so, thanks in great measure to women like Susan B. Anthony who took up the gauntlet of women's rights and never laid it down. Susan saw the many injustices and inequalities that women faced and felt deeply that these things must be changed. To her, a woman's lot in life was, plainly and simply, unfair. Other people, both women and men, saw the same things she did but never questioned them; they felt that what existed was the natural order of things.

Susan Anthony worked for all the great human-rights struggles of her time, but more than any other person she was responsible for organizing the women's movement—training its leaders and directing it toward its special goal of obtaining the vote for women, and also for its more ambitious plan of equality for women in all areas of life.

An incident that occurred when Susan was eleven illustrates how even a young girl can have her eyes opened. Susan's father owned a mill that employed a number of young women. One of them, Sally Ann, was the mill's most efficient weaver. She was also skilled at maintenance. When the yarn became tangled or the machinery broke down, Elijah, the overseer, would inevitably ask Sally to find the trouble and fix it. One day, Susan reasonably asked her father, "If Sally Ann knows more about weaving than Elijah, why don't you make her the overseer?" Although Daniel Anthony was more progressive than most men of his time, his answer was distinctly traditional: "It would never do to have a woman overseer in the mill."

Why should the person most capable be denied a job just because of her sex? This was a question that Susan would ponder for years.

Susan Brownell Anthony was born on February 15, 1820, in Adams, Massachusetts, a small village nestled at the foot of Mount Greylock in the scenic Berkshire Hills. As a very little girl she would watch the sun set over "Old Greylock" and imagined that the mountain peak was the highest spot in the world, the place where the earth touched the sky. Susan was the second child and the second daughter born to the Anthonys. She had the very good fortune to be born into a family that encouraged its members to think for themselves.

Daniel Anthony came from a long line of Quakers. In fact, the family had been Quakers since the religion was introduced in America during the mid-seventeenth century. The Quakers, or Society of Friends as their official title proclaimed them, were noted for their sobriety in speech and dress, but Daniel had a strong streak of liberalism in him. This probably came from his family who were wealthy and a little too worldly for some of their fellow parishioners' taste. Even though Daniel's mother, Hannah, wore the simple Quaker styles, the material was of the finest quality and all her hats were made in New York. Her husband, Humphrey, could well afford these luxuries. He was an ambitious man who owned farms, cattle, and orchards and was always searching for ways to acquire more.

Daniel, the oldest of nine children, grew up in comfortable surroundings within the sight of Mount Greylock. By the time he was a young man he had the reputation of following "the inner light," a Quaker term for a person's conscience. Until he was eighteen he alternately worked for his father and attended a local school, but Hannah had high educational aspirations for her son. Learning that a new Quaker boarding school was opening, she persuaded Humphrey to send Daniel to Nine Partners in New York.

This progressive Quaker institution had a strong effect on Daniel. He did some teaching during his last year there and wished to stay on in that capacity. But his father wanted him to work in the family business, and ordered him to come home.

So Daniel, now a good-looking young man of twenty with snapping black eyes, returned. He helped his father with the farming business, but in his spare time taught small classes for neighborhood young people. One of his students was Lucy Read.

Lucy and Daniel had known each other years before when they were both students at a local public school. Mainly, he remembered her as the playmate of his younger sister; but now he found she was grown up, and it was not long before they fell in love. There was one major problem, however. Lucy was not a Quaker.

Lucy Read's family had lived in Massachusetts since before the Revolutionary War, and her father, Daniel Read, had fought in it, earning commendations for his bravery. She spent an unusually happy childhood playing with her sister Avis in a farm that adjoined the Anthonys'. Her parents were well matched, although Daniel Read left the Baptist church, much to his wife's chagrin, and joined the Universalists, a liberal sect that did not believe in Hell. Mrs. Read said she wore her knees out praying for him, but he died a happy Universalist at the age of eighty-eight.

Lucy thought long and hard before marrying Daniel Anthony. She adored pretty clothes, parties, and dancing, all of which she would have to give up if she married a Quaker as the religion forbade that sort of frivolity. Nevertheless, love won out, and on July 13, 1817, they were married in a quiet civil ceremony.

Susan herself, years later, termed the romance "pretty adventurous" and told how Lucy, in anticipation of a quiet married life, had demanded one last fling. She attended a dancing party where she whirled across the floor with different partners while Daniel waited patiently to take her home. It was four in the morning before she was ready to leave.

Daniel had his own problems with the marriage. He was the first Anthony for generations to marry outside the religion and he was called in by the church elders to discuss this transgression. He simply told them that Lucy was the woman he loved, and because of his sincerity (and perhaps because his father was so generous to the church) they let him remain a member.

Lucy did not become a Quaker, fearing that she could not live up to the religion's strict standards. She did, however, dress more simply and gave up many of her favorite pastimes, including singing. Every so often she would backslide long enough to sing her children a lullaby, but she had to endure her in-laws' displeasure when they heard her.

Though not an official Quaker, Lucy would often accompany her family to meetings, and eventually all the Anthony children were taken into the church. The Quakers stressed the equality of men and women, something that was unique in religious circles. Susan would sit in the simple Quaker meeting house and see her grandmother, Hannah Lapham Anthony, occupying the "high seat" as an elder of the church. She could also listen to one of her aunts preaching as members were encouraged to do when the spirit so moved them. Young Susan naturally assumed that the opinions of women were respected everywhere as they were in her church.

Daniel Anthony, who once had wished to be a teacher, became an energetic, enterprising businessman. Within the first years of Susan's life, he had built a cotton mill using a little stream which flowed through the Read farm for water power. The mill was built to meet what would become a steady demand for cotton cloth which was just coming into use and considered quite a luxury. But as a Quaker, Daniel opposed slavery and he tried not to buy raw cotton that had been raised by slaves. He also frowned upon drinking and formed a temperance society among his workers, making them promise to abstain from alcohol. Later, when he opened a company store, he refused to sell liquor there though most stores of this kind usually did. The abolition of slavery and temperance, the prohibition of alcoholic beverages, were the causes to which the liberals and reformers of that time rallied, and there is no doubt that her father's dedication to these causes influenced Susan at an early age.

Lucy Anthony probably had sympathy for these causes too, but this was not the primary message Susan received from her mother. After her marriage, Lucy became withdrawn. Her gaiety was stifled by constant household tasks, and her continual pregnancies (eight in all) seemed to her a reason for shame.

In addition to her regular housekeeping duties, once Daniel got his mill going, Lucy was responsible for the mill girls who came down from the mountains to work in the factory. Before the industrial revolution, few women had a chance to earn their own money. Then, in the 1820s and 1830s, after the invention of the spinning jenny and power loom, textile mills sprang up all over New England. It soon became obvious that women, already familiar with the techniques of spinning, were well suited for this work and they flocked to the factories. Surprisingly, no one objected much to women moving to mill towns as long as they were well chaperoned. They were already making cloth at home and mill work seemed an extension of spinning and a temporary one at that. Some of the women workers were the daughters of poor farmers and they fully expected to return home and get married after they had earned some money. Others were young widows who needed to support themselves, and still others were girls sent down to help finance the education of a male family member.

Many young women who wanted to enter the mills had to convince their fathers that they would not be tempted by the freedom of being away from home. Mill owners, who needed this cheap labor, responded by providing respectable housing arrangements for their workers. Those who worked in the Anthony factory were divided between Daniel's sister's house and his own. Lucy did all the cooking, cleaning and washing for her eleven boarders and took care of three little children at the same time. In her biography, Susan says that although her father was a generous man who loved his wife and could afford help, it probably never even occurred to him that this burden might be too much for Lucy. Even if he had suggested it, she goes on to say, Lucy would probably have resented the implication that she could not handle the load. She was doing what women were expected to do.

Susan was only a little girl during the mill days in Adams, and since the women were out working from six A.M. to six P.M. every day but Sunday, she saw little of them. Perhaps one reason Lucy did not ask for help was that she quickly got her daughters doing chores as soon as their small hands were able. Susan began by wiping dishes and progressed to setting the table. By the time she was six she could fix a dinner pail and at ten she could prepare a whole dinner.

Susan, her older sister Guelma, and her younger sister Hannah were each only eighteen months apart, making them close enough in age to have a lot of fun together. In spite of Daniel's prospering business, there were no fancy toys, but the girls enjoyed playing with their rag dolls and a set of cast-off dishes. They delighted in going to their Grandmother Anthony's house where they stuffed themselves with maple candy, doughnuts, and all kinds of home-baked goodies. Susan especially loved her grandmother's cooking. According to family folklore, when Lucy chided her daughter for eating at her grandmother's what she could get at home, Susan impudently replied, "Why Grandma's potato peelings are better than your boiled dinners."

One unfortunate incident involving Lucy made a lasting impression on the sensitive young girl. When Susan was three, she and her sister Guelma were sent to her grandmother's while Lucy awaited the birth of her fourth child who, as it turned out, was stillborn. Susan contracted whooping cough during her stay, so her visit was extended. During her convalescence Susan was taught by a cousin to read, and she could hardly wait to get home to show off her new skill. Instead of a happy homecoming, Susan was greeted by a horrified mother who noticed immediately that her daughter's once lovely dark eyes now turned inward toward her nose. The affliction seemed to have been the result of her illness possibly complicated by her efforts to read.

Perhaps because of her recent tragedy, Lucy over-reacted. She was extremely depressed about Susan's appearance and took every opportunity to tell her so. The right eye eventually straightened out, but Susan was always self-conscious about her looks. After seventeen years of embarrassment, Susan heard about an operation that might correct the other eye, and her father took her to a nearby town where the surgery was performed. Susan's hopes that her affliction might be corrected were dashed when the doctor removed the bandages. He had cut the muscle too much, and now, instead of turning inward, the eye moved too far to the left. Susan was devastated. Later pictures show her to be an extremely handsome woman with patrician features and her mother's glossy dark hair, but Susan considered herself an ugly duckling and insisted on having photographs taken only of her right side. She even took to wearing her mother's spectacles, though they were of no practical use to her.

If Lucy Anthony was reserved and reticent with her children, Daniel was a delightful companion and Susan reveled in being his favorite child. He adored his daughter's quick mind and encouraged her educational endeavors as well as her other pursuits. Daniel's business continued to flourish and in 1826 he moved his family to Battenville, forty-four miles away, where he had been offered a chance to manufacture cotton on a large scale. Lucy was not very happy about leaving her parents, but Daniel felt this was a business opportunity he could not pass up.

Because Daniel (and also Lucy) had received a good education, he felt it was extremely important that his children have the same opportunity. Once they were settled in Battenville, Susan began attending the district school where she was an avid reader and an excellent student. She particularly wanted to learn long division, but the male schoolmaster did not know how to teach it, and probably felt there was no reason for a girl to learn it. Long division was considered a subject strictly for boys! She learned it anyway from a fellow student, but the indifferent teaching made Daniel realize that if his children (who now numbered five) were going to get a better education, he would have to provide it himself.

Daniel and his partner, Judge McLean, had just finished building a new brick store and a room was set aside for the students, including Judge McLean's son, Aaron.

Later, the school was moved to a new wing of the Anthony house and it became the first school in the area to have individual seats for each student. These were only stools, but they were considered to be a great improvement over the bench that ran along the sides of the old schoolroom, an uncomfortable place to sit all day.

Daniel's love of learning extended to his mill workers and he started evening classes for them. Some he taught himself while others were conducted by the children's teacher. The classes were very popular and the good turnout was probably spontaneous. He took special care in choosing his teachers and he seemed to continually place competent young women in that position. Two early teachers were educated Quaker cousins who fit in well with the family. Later, a more worldly teacher was hired, who wanted to attend the village sings. Lucy felt it was all right, but Daniel did not. He thought that if the teacher sang it would be a bad influence on his children.

Susan was enrolled in the Society of Friends when she was thirteen years old. Until then, the family had attended services, but only Daniel was an actual member. One cold, blustery day Daniel decided to go alone to the meeting but Susan tagged along with him. She knew women were not allowed to stay in the main room during the business meeting, but since that was the warmest part of the building, she sneaked behind the stove and curled up there. One of the elders found her and asked if she was a member.

"No, but my father is," replied Susan.

"That will not do, thee will have to go out."

"My mother told me to stay in."

"Thy mother does not manage things here."

Susan tried to tell the elder that her father, a true member, also wanted her inside, but she soon found herself being firmly deposited in the freezing hallway. She decided to go to a neighbor's house to warm up and there the family's large dog sprang at her, taking a giant rip out of her new plaid coat.

Both Lucy and Daniel were upset by the whole incident

and decided to request that all their children, even baby Mary, be enrolled in the church so that nothing like this would ever happen again. When she was an old woman, Susan laughingly said that the reason she became a Quaker was so that she would not be forced out into the snow.

These preteenage years were a busy time for Susan. She had her schoolwork, the never-ending chores, and one pastime at which she excelled—needlework. A sampler she made when she was eleven still exists today. In crewel, she carefully stitched her family tree and surrounded it with a wreath of strawberries.

She even worked briefly in the mill. Now that she was older, Susan was fascinated by the mill workings. She envied the girls who worked there, many of whom were not much older than herself. When Susan heard that one of the spoolers had been taken ill, Susan and Hannah both begged to take the girl's place. Lucy did not like the idea at all, but Daniel was pleased by his daughters' interest and thought one of them should have a chance. Finally, Lucy gave her grudging consent and the two girls drew lots for the job with the understanding that whoever won would split the wages with the other. Susan, the excited winner, spent the next two weeks skillfully and deftly tending the spools. For her work she received the standard wages of three dollars.

STUDENT AND TEACHER

2

All the care and attention that Daniel poured into his daughter's schooling was highly unusual for the times. Most girls were given the bare essentials of an education and whether or not females should be educated at all was a topic of much debate in the seventeenth, eighteenth and even nineteenth centuries.

Those against educating women said learning would be wasted on these frivolous, empty-headed creatures. Their opponents argued that women could not expect to be much else when they were denied an education. Once women would acquire an education and training they could develop their abilities and no longer be limited to the role of homemaker for a husband and children.

This, of course, was exactly what some people were afraid of. Education seemed the first step toward forsaking women's traditional roles as wives and mothers. Critics even warned that study would be too difficult for delicate females and that their minds and bodies would be so damaged it would affect their childbearing. Even the noted liberal philosopher Jean Jacques Rousseau wrote that "the education of women should always be relative to men. . . . The woman is formed expressly to please the man." Ironically, Rousseau was best known for his writings promoting freedom of the individual. By individuals he obviously meant men.

If most people were opposed to education, particularly higher education, for women, they were horrified by the idea of young men and women attending school together. They protested this practice on two levels. First, putting boys and girls in the same classroom would almost lead inevitably to licentious behavior. There was also the matter of women's inferior brains. Everyone knew that females could not keep up intellectually with males, so having them in the same class would mean that educational standards would lower.

This inequality was strongly supported by America's religious institutions. Preachers quoted the Bible as proof that women were inferior to men and insisted that one of their punishments for Eve's sin was continual deference to their husbands' needs and judgments. Even when things began changing during the nineteenth century, organized religions were among the last social institutions to approve of it. The one religious group that not only encouraged but insisted upon the education of women was the Quakers. When Daniel went off to Nine Partners School, his sisters went with him.

Susan's excellent home education was put to good use when, at fifteen, she began teaching during summers at her family's Battenville school. Soon after, she boarded out as a teacher with a Quaker family that lived in a nearby town. All three of the older Anthony girls did this, and though it was considered peculiar in some circles for a successful man to send his daughters out to teach, Daniel Anthony felt it was of the utmost importance that the girls be able to support themselves should the need arise.

But just because Susan had been out on her own as a teacher did not mean her own education was finished. It was the custom for wealthy families to send their children to boarding schools and Daniel was certain this was in keeping with his family's station. Moreover, there was now at least some choice of where girls could continue their studies.

Women's education took a leap forward in 1821 when Emma Willard opened the Troy Female Academy. As a girl Emma had shown a real inclination for mathematics, a talent her father encouraged. But when it was time for her to continue her education, there was no school that was willing to accept a woman. So Emma studied on her own and after a great fund-raising effort opened a school for women in Troy, New York.

In 1836 Daniel received notice of another women's seminary opening, this one in Philadelphia. Deborah Moulson's Seminary for Females had as its aim the fostering of "moral discipline, simplicity of speech, behavior, and apparel." Its courses included the basic "three R's," as well as a few unusual subjects such as philosophy, chemistry, and astronomy. Coming as she did from a Quaker background, Deborah Moulson inspired confidence in Daniel, who sent seventeen-year-old Guelma to her when the school opened. She was followed by Susan a year later. The cost for each girl was $125 per year.

Traveling all the way to Philadelphia was an exciting event for Susan. She loved listening to Daniel's accounts of his business travels, and now, headed for the big city on a wagon and steamboat, she could hardly believe that she was out in the world. Guelma had sent back glowing reports of the school and Susan expected to like it there every bit as much as her sister did.

But almost as soon as she was left at the school by her father, Susan began to feel homesick. Guelma's presence did not seem to have been much help to her. Instead, Susan tried to alleviate her loneliness by writing many letters to her family and friends which they dutifully tried to answer.

Even worse than her homesickness was the poor relationship Susan had with Miss Moulson right from the beginning. Guelma was one of the headmistress's pets, but she and Susan kept butting heads. Once, in an angry outburst, Susan accused her teacher of playing favorites. "Thy sister, Guelma, does the best she is capable of," Miss Moulson replied. "Thee has greater abilities and I demand the best of thy capacity." This did not comfort Susan who had been trying hard to win the teacher's approval. Somehow she just could not seem to do anything right.

Susan confided her frustrations to her diary. In one incident she reported that the teacher chastised her for not dotting her *i*'s properly; in another, she was punished for sending a personal letter without first letting Miss Moulson check it for grammar and spelling. Her worst indiscretion, however, was accidentally damaging her teacher's desk. Susan was trying to help Miss Moulson by cleaning out some cobwebs the woman had complained about. To get at the ceiling webs, she stepped up on the desk, breaking the lock and bending the hinges. Susan claimed responsibility immediately, but Miss Moulson, pretending she did not know who had done it, humiliated the guilty party in front of the whole class. In her biography written over sixty years later, Susan said that she could never recall the incident without feeling ill.

From all reports, Miss Moulson was unduly harsh with the girl but Susan took most of the blame for their disagreements on herself and it left the impressionable girl quite sad. Susan, always insecure, was particularly vulnerable to Miss Moulson's type of psychological punishment. One of the teacher's favorite ploys was to accuse unnamed students of doing this or that. Susan inevitably felt the headmistress was talking about her, even when she had some other student in mind. Later it was learned that the woman was suffering from consumption, a serious disease of the time from which she died not long after. Perhaps her illness was the reason for her uncharitable behavior.

It was at the seminary that Susan, by now eighteen, began to have her first friendships with boys. Despite her problems with her teacher, she had great affection for Miss Moulson's brother, John, who was almost the same age as Susan. She also kept up a lively correspondence with her old Battenville friend, Aaron McLean, who kept her posted on all the news from home. Susan's first recorded view of marriage was written in her diary in response to Aaron's news that a mutual friend was marrying a widower with five children. She wrote, "I think any female would rather live and die an old maid."

But if life was not happy at the Moulson Seminary, even darker clouds were gathering on the home front. The whole country was in the midst of a depression and Daniel's business had been severely affected. By the spring of 1838, Susan and her sister returned home to the news that the family's assets had been attached by Daniel's creditors and that all their possessions were to be sold at public auction to pay off his debts.

Susan was away teaching to earn some money at the time of auction, but she received a full description of how not only Daniel's but Lucy's, his wife's, possessions were auctioned off. Her prized cotton sheets, silver spoons, personal clothing and underwear, and even her family Bible were put up for bidding. Luckily for the Anthonys, Lucy's brother Joshua Read came to town to bid on his sister's belongings and he did manage to salvage some of them. Nevertheless, the lesson of all this must have been clear to Susan—a woman owned nothing that could not be sold to pay her husband's debts.

Daniel's financial setbacks caused the family to move from their comfortable house in Battenville to a rented tavern in the nearby town of Hardscrabble. The tavern, once a popular hostel, was no longer in the center of town commerce, but whenever an odd traveler did show up, the Anthonys took him in in order to earn a little money. There was also a small mill on the land that Daniel hoped to expand but this plan came to nothing. The family was kept alive primarily by the salaries Guelma and Susan earned as teachers. Daniel kept strict accounts of how much his daughters were donating; he was determined to repay them when he got back on his feet. Despite all their hardship, many members of the Anthony family remembered this as a happy time when they worked together and supported each other emotionally and financially.

After trying various vocational dead ends, including running his own school, Daniel moved to Rochester, New York,

Brandywine Senior High Library

Niles, Michigan

where he once more prospered, first as a farmer, then as a businessman with the New York Life Insurance Company. But this took a number of years, and in the intervening time, Susan felt that it was necessary to pursue her teaching career with as much vigor as she could. As soon as one job ended, she found another somewhere else.

In New Rochelle, New York, Susan taught at a boarding school, and in her next job, closer to home in Center Falls, she had a chance to show how much she had learned about controlling a class. One big bully thought that a young teacher would be an easy mark for his shenanigans. Susan tried reason, then threats, and finally had to take him out in back and use a cane. He fought viciously but at last she subdued him and he caused no further problems. Other potential troublemakers were held in check, too. Susan's teaching skills improved with each job she took but her payment always stayed the same, ranging from $2.00 to $2.50 a week. She was usually replacing an inefficient man who had just been dismissed for incompetence, but her wages were only a fourth of what his had been. This was infuriating, as she needed the money for her family as much as any man did.

Each place she moved, Susan had some attention from young men. There were a few whose company she enjoyed, but for the most part she would confide unflattering criticisms of her dates to her diary. When a prosperous middle-aged widower proposed to her, giving as one reason that she reminded him of his first wife, Susan laughed and said she had no desire to be anyone's second. Even her sister Guelma's marriage to her old friend Aaron McLean in 1839 did not make Susan wish for wedding bells. In fact, after sharing such a strong friendship, she and Aaron found themselves less and less on the same wavelength. Even he was developing a demeaning male attitude toward women that Susan was increasingly coming to detest. Once, not long after Aaron and Guelma were married, Susan visited the newlyweds. Proudly, she told them that she had been taking algebra lessons, but Aaron told Susan she was wasting her time. He did approve, however, of the delicious biscuits

Susan had baked for them and ate several, saying, "I'd rather see a woman make biscuits like this than solve the knottiest problems in algebra." Susan retorted, "There's no reason she shouldn't do both!"

In 1846, through the help of her Uncle Joshua Read, Susan obtained a job as girl's headmistress at the Canajoharie Academy in New York. She lived with her cousin, Margaret, Uncle Joshua's daughter, and while the job had more prestige than her former ones, she was still making only as much as she had earned in Battenville years before.

By now Susan was in her mid-twenties. Since her father was finally doing well with his Rochester area farm, Susan, for the first time in her teaching career, began to spend some money on herself. Though she was to declare in later life that she always considered herself a Quaker, it was at this time, too, that she began to drop some of the trappings of Quakerism. She banished the "thees" and "thous" of Quaker speech and started wearing brighter colors. She became very interested in fashion, read the popular journal *Godey's Lady's Book* whenever she could get her hands on a copy. She did not have enough spare money to buy jewelry, but her cousins were quite generous about lending her theirs. She did buy many clothes, however, and carefully noted in her diary the cost and description of everything she wore including a fox muff for eight dollars and a mantilla that cost thirty! Once, after an important board examination, she wrote more about her new purple plaid muslin dress with the puffed sleeves than she did about the questions she was asked to answer.

On the social side, she continued her outings with gentlemen callers, but now she was ready to try some very unQuakerlike pursuits. She went to the circus, on long drives, and even to dances. She still did not like drinking, however, and one incident, which may have played a part in her zeal for the temperance movement, concerned an escort who perhaps offended her in some way. She wrote to her sister, Mary, "I shall certainly not attend another dance unless I can have a total abstinence man to accompany me and not one

Susan B. Anthony in 1848, at the time
she was teaching at Canajoharie Academy

whose highest delight is to make a fool of himself." It did not bother her to be at a dance, she continued, but she heartily disliked the "brandy-sipping."

If a less-staid Susan was sedately sowing some wild oats, she was also involved with her career. She did very well on her first quarterly examination in front of the principal, trustees, and parents. They were impressed with her knowledge, and apparently her looks as well, because everyone said, "The schoolmarm looked quite beautiful." She may have appreciated the compliment, but it continued to irk Susan that women teachers were so discriminated against in terms of status and salary.

Years later, this issue was still bothering her. She was attending a teacher's convention at the time and rose to speak about the lack of respect for the teaching profession as a whole. Even though three-quarters of the teachers in the audience were women, they were not allowed access to the podium and Susan's request to make a statement aroused the group. The question of whether a woman should be allowed to speak had to be introduced by a man, and then it was fiercely debated. After she won the right to speak by a small margin, Susan told the convention exactly why teachers did not get much respect.

"It seems to me," she said, "you fail to comprehend the cause of disrespect of which you complain. Do you not see that so as society says women have not brains enough to be a doctor or a lawyer or a minister, but has plenty to be a teacher, many of you who condescend to teach tacitly admit . . . he has no more brains than a woman." No doubt some members of the audience thought that rather than allowing women into medicine or law, it might be best to eliminate them from teaching.

Susan continued to teach from time to time all her life, but after she left her post in Canajoharie, she turned in a different direction. There were several reasons why she gave up this rather prestigious position.

Her cousin Margaret, with whom she had been living, died and Susan blamed her death, in part, on the neglect shown to Margaret by her husband. As their boarder, Susan had observed this marriage at first hand and it reinforced her notion that marriage favored men and worked against women. She wrote to her mother that unless there was some strong emotional tie, there was no reason to be married. This was certainly not the opinion of most women of Susan's age. Unmarried women in their late twenties were usually more than willing to make a marriage of convenience.

Within a few weeks after Margaret's death, a new principal, one more rigid and harsher than his predecessor, arrived at the school. This unpleasant young man was from the South where his father was a slaveholder. Susan was so firmly against slavery that the thought of working for someone with proslavery viewpoints made her angry.

Even with these reasons for leaving, it must have been a hard decision for Susan to make. If she were a man she could have gone West, where the Gold Rush was starting; she said going to California was her dream. But as a woman without a job, all she could do was go home.

Still, she had become active in temperance work fighting the evils of alcohol while she lived in Canajoharie, and she was well aware of the abolitionists' work to free the slaves. Her sympathies certainly were with these causes. Perhaps, she thought, she could turn her energies to the growing reform movements.

CAUSES

3

The first women's rights convention was held in Seneca Falls, New York, during the summer of 1848. The gathering sprang from an idea five women had while they were sitting drinking tea in the home of Jane Hunt. Lucretia Mott, a Quaker preacher, her sister Martha C. Wright, and Mary Ann McClintock sat listening to the fifth woman, Elizabeth Cady Stanton, describe how unhappy she was in her traditional role of wife and mother. Earlier, Mrs. Stanton had lived a stimulating life in Boston where she had been involved in various reform movements, from abolition to organizations promoting the elimination of wars. Now she lived in Seneca Falls, a small town in upstate New York, and felt frustrated at being unable to use either her talent or her intelligence.

The other women to whom she poured out these feelings sympathized completely. The more they talked about the injustices that women faced, the more they decided that something must be done. So, as was the custom in the reform movements of the day, they decided to call a convention. There they would discuss the myriad problems and discriminations that women faced.

That very night they wrote a newspaper advertisement calling on women to attend "A convention to discuss the social, civil and religious conditions and rights of women at the Wesleyan Chapel at Seneca Falls on the 19th and 20th of July." The announcement ran on July 14th, 1848, in the *Seneca County Courier*. This gave the women a week to make some plans. When they placed the notice, they had very little idea about what form the meeting would take. All they knew was that Lucretia Mott and Elizabeth Cady Stanton would speak.

The next day the five met at Mary Ann McClintock's home. Sitting around a desk that is now in the Smithsonian Institution, they decided the first order of business was to draw up a statement, something that would synthesize all their concerns. They fumbled with the form at first, but at last they chose to base their document on the Declaration of Independence; theirs was to be called A Declaration of Sentiments.

So that people would understand the similarity between the two Declarations, the women used the same phraseology to make their point. In the sentence that begins, "We hold these truths to be self evident . . ." they changed the wording to read, "that all men *and women* are created equal." They listed the many social, legal, and moral injustices that women had to endure, and the preamble ended with the demand that women receive all the rights and privileges that belonged to them as citizens of the United States.

Elizabeth Cady Stanton then set to work drawing up specific resolutions that could be put to practical use in fighting inequality between the sexes while at the same time opening women's eyes to the unfairness of their status. The most shocking resolution was the ninth, the one demanding the right to vote: "Resolved that it is the duty of the women of the country to secure to themselves their sacred right to the elective franchise."

Mrs. Stanton's husband, Henry, was a liberal lawyer who encouraged her work in this area, but the resolution for women's suffrage was too much even for him and he demanded that she remove it. Even Lucretia Mott, no stranger to controversy, thought that by asking for the vote, Elizabeth was moving too far, too fast. But Elizabeth absolutely refused to budge and the ninth resolution stayed in.

The day of the conference, wagonloads of women descended on Seneca Falls. At first the organizers had trouble opening the church, which someone, perhaps purposely, had locked from the inside, but eventually the three hundred women and forty men were let inside. It was lucky that a few sympathetic men did show up. Since it was unheard of for a woman to chair any sort of public meeting, Lucretia Mott's husband, James, presided.

There were speeches, debates, and finally the vote on the Declaration of Sentiments. Most of the provisions passed easily, but the ninth resolution advocating women's suffrage caused a furious debate. Finally, after a ringing speech by former slave and abolitionist Frederick Douglass, the resolution passed.

This convention was the official beginning of the women's movement in the United States. Its organizers were astounded by its success, but one woman not there to witness the triumph was Susan B. Anthony.

Susan was still teaching at Canajoharie in 1848 and the issue of women's rights was not one of her priorities. Most people found the convention shocking; newspapers railed against it, calling it a "petticoat rebellion" and an "unnatural incident." Susan probably gave it little thought either way, choosing to direct her energies toward the abolition of liquor and slavery. Despite the injustices she had suffered at the hands of men, Susan had not felt discrimination the way many women had. She had received a good education, had access to her own money, and was beholden to no man. A narrow Married Woman's Property Law had been passed by the New York legislature. It made illegal such situations as that endured by Lucy Anthony when her belongings were put on the auction block, a minor bit of progress that was a comfort to Susan. It would be at least four years before women's rights would be added to her agenda. Now, in true Anthony tradition, her main cause was temperance.

Daniel Anthony had long been interested in the temperance movement. In the early days of the Adams mill, his company store had sold spirits like the other merchants in the area. Then he heard a tragic story about a man who had frozen to death by the side of the road, clutching a liquor bottle. Obviously, he had become unconscious while drunk and never woke up. Daniel was horrified by this tale. Then and there he stopped selling liquor in his store and refused to do so in Battenville, even when his partner, Judge McLean, told him the mill workers would rise up if it were not provided. They did not, and Daniel went a step further, asking the men to take a pledge against drinking alcohol. Many did, and Daniel took a personal interest in their progress. Elijah, his Battenville foreman, had a drinking problem and finally Daniel had to let him go because of it. Feeling almost as unhappy as his employee, he had one last talk with Elijah and agreed to give him his job back if he promised never to drink again. Elijah was so inspired and grateful, he never touched another drop.

Drinking had long been accepted as a part of American culture. Homemade whisky, hard cider, and rum were the drinks of the common man, while those who could afford it drank imported liquors and wines. Alcohol was often prescribed by doctors for a variety of ailments, and children were just as likely to get a dose as older patients.

The Puritans, America's early settlers, drank some alcohol, but drinking really took hold in the country when immigrants from nations that had a strong history of alcohol consumption settled in the United States. They brought with them an acceptance of drinking that made the use of alcoholic beverages so prevalent that many people thought it was out of control.

Dr. Benjamin Rush was the first to advocate the idea of temperance, in the late 1700s. In 1808 he wrote a pamphlet about intoxication that started people thinking about the effects of drinking on American society. Many people thought such ills as decaying morality, physical weakness, and an increase in crime stemmed from drinking and they were determined that America would be a better country without alcohol. These people formed the nucleus of the temperance movement which gained momemtum in the early 1800s.

By 1830, groups calling themselves the Sons of Temperance were springing up all over America. Women, too, had a great stake in seeing their men sober. Drunken husbands were dangerous and used family food money to indulge their habit, so naturally women wanted to join and lend their support to the temperance groups. At first they were rebuffed by the male members, who thought a woman's participation in such a cause was unladylike, but finally women organized their own auxiliaries, the Daughters of Temperance, and grudgingly the men came to accept their help. Soon it became socially acceptable for a woman to belong to the local temperance society, and since this was one of the few outlets for women outside the home, the number of such societies grew.

With Daniel's interest in temperance, it is not surprising that Susan threw herself into the cause quite early. When she arrived in Canajoharie, she found it already had a chapter of Daughters of Temperance and soon she became its president. She was able to use her excellent fund-raising abilities and even made a speech before the people of the village about the temperance cause. This was a bold action for the time; public speaking by a woman was considered unfeminine at the very least and probably unnatural. But with her strong memories of women speaking out in church, Susan felt it a duty to express herself on this issue. Her sincere effort was received warmly, much to her surprise.

A copy of this speech is still preserved in the Library of Congress. It is written in her own hand on pages she sewed together and for which she made a cover. Her comments are a justification for women to involve themselves in the temperance cause: ". . . Who is to urge on this vast work of reform? Shall it not be those aggrieved by the foul destroyer's inroads? Then arises the question, how are we to accomplish the end desired? I answer, not by confining our influence to our home circle." These words may sound old-fashioned to the modern ear, but this clarion call to women, urging them out into the field, could not have been more advanced at the time.

Another great movement of the nineteenth century was for the abolition of slavery. Today one might think that all Northerners wanted to see the slaves freed. This was not the case. Many felt that a strong economy was based on the cheap labor of the slaves and they wanted to keep the system. Others, who called themselves abolitionists, proposed gradual or limited emancipation. Still others wanted to let the Southerners continue to own slaves but opposed the extension of slavery into the Western states. The most radical fringe of abolitionists belonged to the American Anti-slavery Society. This group was organized in 1833 by Wiliam Lloyd Garrison, a liberal newspaper editor and reformer, and they demanded immediate and unconditional emancipation of all the slaves in the United States and its territories. Many prominent people of the day belonged to the Anti-slavery Society but the group as a whole was not popular and was viewed by most people as troublemakers.

As in the temperance movement, women were only reluctantly allowed to become antislavery workers. Only when the need for help became so great that men could not do all the jobs were women invited to become active in the many abolition groups of the day.

Susan's family and their friends had planted the seeds of abolition in her at an early age. As a very little girl, Susan first saw black people in Battenville. Her younger sister, Hannah, was frightened of them, but Susan's primary emotion was pity when her father explained to her that these people could be bought and sold like cattle. At the Moulson Academy, Susan heard much about the abolition movement from Lydia Mott, a teacher who was related to Lucretia Mott. When Susan was in New Rochelle, she disapprovingly observed the rude and insensitive attitude her fellow Quakers there had toward blacks. In one instance, the sight of a polite, well-dressed black man sitting in the meeting caused a number of worshipers to walk out. Another time, three visiting black girls accustomed to attending Friends' meetings in their home towns were not allowed to sit downstairs but were sent up to the gallery instead. An indignant Susan took great pleasure in inviting them to tea and she was especially nice to them when they met in church.

At the same time, Daniel Anthony was becoming more and more involved in the movement and by the early 1840s the Anthony home had become a meeting place for abolitionists. Frederick Douglass, the escaped slave who eventually bought his freedom, had begun publishing a newspaper called *The North Star*, which was read avidly by all the Anthonys. Eventually Douglass and William Lloyd Garrison found their way to the Anthony house and the family was considered a part of the liberal group of abolitionists known as the Garrisonians.

By 1850 Susan had left her teaching post at Canajoharie to live with her family in Rochester. Daniel was now spending time with his flourishing insurance business, so Susan took over some of the planting and harvesting jobs on the farm. She was also present when these famous and powerful men came to her house, and just listening to them discuss their lofty goals inspired her.

The year 1850 also saw passage of a harsh law against runaway slaves and those who harbored them. But rather than scaring abolitionists, the law welded them together even more tightly and Rochester became a major stop on the escape route for slaves called the "underground railway," which helped the runaways get to freedom in Canada. The issue of slavery also caused the Anthony family to break with the Quakers in Rochester, many of whom were not abolitionists. This was, of course, a difficult decision for the family, but they felt so strongly that the slaves must be freed, they began attending the Unitarian Church, which was more in sympathy with their cause.

As Susan quickly learned, people who were active in one reform movement were often involved in the others. Susan learned from the people who came to the farm about the women's struggle and when the first National Women's Rights Convention was held in Worcester, Massachusetts, in the fall of 1850, she read with great interest the account of the proceedings. Still, she was not ready to take a stand on this reform movement.

Daniel, however, had been a supporter of women's rights for at least two years. After the Seneca Falls convention, another convention had been called in Rochester, two weeks later. Susan's father, sister, and rather surprisingly, her mother, had not only attended but had signed petitions in favor of the resolutions and sentiments. It astonished Susan that her father, who had never voted in elections because his Quaker religion regarded it wrong to support a government that believed in war nevertheless supported the right of women to vote. Susan, who at the time was still living in Canajoharie, was so unattuned to the women's movement, that upon hearing of their participation, wrote them a letter chiding them for getting ahead of the times.

By the time of the 1850 convention in Rochester, of course, Susan had become informed on the issue of women's rights. People she knew such as William Garrison and Frederick Douglass had convinced her that the women's cause was a just one. From these people she also heard about those working within the women's movement—among them the motherly yet shrewd Elizabeth Cady Stanton and the independent Lucy Stone. These women intrigued Susan and she was eager to meet them. But she certainly had no idea that they would soon be working side by side.

FRIENDS

4

Susan Anthony might never have moved wholeheartedly into the women's movement if she had not met Elizabeth Cady Stanton. Susan first heard about Mrs. Stanton from her family. Her impassioned plea for women's suffrage at the Rochester convention in 1848 had convinced them to sign her petitions. Anyone who could impress the Anthony family that much was of great interest to Susan.

Who was this leading light of the women's movement? Then (and sometimes even today) people viewed feminists as rabid, ill-humored, man-hating females. Elizabeth Cady Stanton could not have been farther from this stereotype. Born in 1815, she described herself in her autobiography, as a "plump little girl with very fair skin, rosy cheeks, good features, dark brown hair and laughing eyes." She was just as attractive and merry as an adult.

Her parents were kind but strict as was usual at that time. Even as a child she felt constrained by the customs of the era and she once inquired of her harsh Scottish nurse why everything that was fun was considered a sin while all the drudgery seemed commanded by God. Needless to say, her nurse was duly shocked that a child would even wonder about such a thing, much less question it aloud. Actually, Elizabeth and her sister, Mary, concocted an ingenious plan to overcome the everlasting no's they heard. They decided to do what they wanted, and while they would probably be punished for their actions, at least they would have had the fun.

Young Elizabeth's life was deeply affected by the death of her older brother, the only boy in the family. Judge Cady, Elizabeth's father, was so distraught over the loss that Elizabeth vowed then and there to become the boy her father no longer had. She studied continuously, rode horses, played games, and did everything she could to make her father say "You're just as good as any boy." Instead, her accomplishments only spurred him to say that it was too bad she was not a boy.

With so much of her energy directed toward trying to impress her father, and aided by her innate cleverness and intellect, it is no surprise that Elizabeth became an excellent student. As soon as she was old enough she attended Emma Willard's Troy Female Academy; afterward she would have liked to have continued her education but no colleges that granted degrees were open to women. Instead, she studied law with her father, but this was purely for her own pleasure. There was no way she could become a lawyer because women were not allowed to take the bar exam.

The pretty child Elizabeth grew into a handsome, dimpled woman who wore her curls on top of her head. She had many admirers but considered her men friends adversaries as well. She loved to argue with them, especially about equality of the sexes, and quickly showed them she could hold her own in any intellectual debate.

If her own inherent views were not liberal enough, they were further radicalized by visits to the home of her cousin, Gerrit Smith. Smith was a well-known reformer and his estate at Peterboro, New York, boasted a spacious mansion that

Elizabeth Cady Stanton at the age of twenty

was also a stop on the underground railway. Everyone seemed to find their way there, from well-known radicals to the Oneida Indians on whose land the estate rested. It was a tradition that because Smith's father had gotten such a good bargain on the grounds, the Indians were entitled to some yearly hospitality.

It was also at Peterboro that Elizabeth first met her future husband, reformer Henry Stanton. One of the most eloquent orators for the abolition movement, Henry cut a dashing figure. They apparently fell in love quickly, but conservative Judge Cady objected to the match, and they broke their engagement. Then Stanton proposed again and Elizabeth decided to accept. One lure may have been that Henry was off to the World Anti-slavery convention in London and Elizabeth wanted very much to attend. After some opposition, they got Judge Cady's grudging consent to the marriage, only to encounter one more stumbling block—Elizabeth would not repeat the marriage vows with the word "obey" in them. Henry, seeing that Elizabeth was not the type to obey anyway, agreed to leave it out.

Despite this independent beginning, Elizabeth went on to become the mother of seven children, and her home life was considered a model of domesticity. In addition to her reform work, Elizabeth often lectured on domestic science and child care.

The fateful meeting between Susan Anthony and Elizabeth Cady Stanton took place on a snowy Seneca Falls street in 1851. With all the reformers increasingly traveling in the same circles, it is not surprising the women met because of an abolitionist meeting. William Lloyd Garrison and the British abolitionist George Thompson were speaking in Seneca Falls, and Susan went there to hear them. She stayed with Amelia Bloomer, whom she knew through her temperance work, and it was Mrs. Bloomer who introduced her to Elizabeth when they all met on the way home from the lecture.

It seems that from their very first meeting Susan and

Mrs. Stanton (as they were always to address each other) felt they were kindred spirits. They soon found out that their skills and talents perfectly meshed. Susan's abilities were attention to detail, her organizational skills, and the way she managed to get any job done efficiently. Elizabeth Stanton was a philosopher whose frustrations, hopes, and aspirations mirrored those of many women, most of whom were not even able to articulate what they felt.

Elizabeth later recalled how at their first meeting she mostly noticed Susan's "good earnest face and genial smile." She invited Susan to visit her, which she soon did. Their meetings become more frequent and while they talked a great deal about temperance and abolition, the plight of women came up often as well.

Susan was greatly moved by the stories Mrs. Stanton told her of her girlhood. Judge Cady often had in his office destitute women who came to him hoping to find a way to get back property or inheritances that greedy husbands had taken for their own. Judge Cady's answers to these women were always the same: "I can't help you, your earnings are his. Your case can't be taken to court because women are not allowed to give evidence."

Little Elizabeth would go through her father's law books and pencil out the unjust laws she heard being discussed. In her child's mind her father was the law, and if she took those laws out of his books they would no longer exist. When Judge Cady explained the legal system to her, he told her that perhaps when she was grown she could petition the government to change the laws she did not like. Rarely has advice given so off-handedly been taken so much to heart. And ironically, when Elizabeth began following her father's advice, he intensely disliked her involvement in the women's cause.

Mrs. Stanton also told Susan about her frustrations closer to home. Her honeymoon trip to the London World Anti-slavery convention was marred by the fact that she and fellow activist Lucretia Mott were not even allowed to participate. If being forced to sit up in a high gallery was not bad enough, they and all the other women delegates had to listen to ministers opposing female participation and scorning their help in the cause. The clergymen buttressed their arguments with ample quotations from the Bible, especially the words of St. Paul, who thought women should be subservient to men.

This was not the first time that Elizabeth had collided with the conventional religious thinkers of the day. As a schoolgirl she had been terrorized by "hell fire and brimstone" preachers and had almost suffered a nervous breakdown because she worried so much about being a sinner. A long family vacation and reading many liberal philosophical books had cleared her head, but it continued to offend her when she heard God's words used as a reason to keep women in their place. Elizabeth's attitude toward the Bible was to have serious repercussions for the movement in later years.

After their honeymoon, the Stantons lived first in her parents' house and later in Boston. Boston suited Elizabeth perfectly. It was a center for reform and liberal thinking and in this charged atmosphere she met and became friends with all kinds of people, including the poets Ralph Waldo Emerson and John Greenleaf Whittier and the novelist Nathaniel Hawthorne. Mrs. Stanton was in an intellectual social whirl. So, it was with regret that when Mr. Stanton's health become too delicate for the harsh Boston winters, the family, which now included three young sons, moved to Seneca Falls in 1847.

Mrs. Stanton found the town provincial on all fronts. Instead of intellectual stimulation, there was household drudgery. Instead of a home with modern conveniences and servants, the family lived in an inefficient, old-fashioned house with no competent maid to be found in the area. But most of all, it seemed unfair that while Mr. Stanton's life went on, filled with business and meetings and travel, her life shrank to taking care of her family. In her own words, "I suffered with a mental hunger which, like an empty stomach, is very depressing." It was this isolation, she told Susan, that led to the planning of the first women's rights convention.

Stories such as these must have set Susan's heart racing, striking a responsive chord in the woman who felt that socially and intellectually she was the equal of any man. Another topic of conversation between the two women was dress reform. When Amelia Bloomer introduced Susan to Mrs. Stanton, Susan couldn't help noticing that the two feminists were wearing similar odd-looking outfits known as the bloomer costume.

Amelia Bloomer, editor of a woman's newspaper, *The Lily*, had not designed the comfortable trousers that were worn under a short skirt. It was Gerrit Smith's daughter who had done that after seeing an outfit that the nurses in Swiss sanitariums wore. But it was Mrs. Bloomer who publicized the costume in her newspaper and eventually it was given her name.

The early feminists felt, with a good deal of justification, that dress reform was an important part of their cause. At the time, a woman's required clothes began with a corset made of steel and whalebone stays, an almost torturous device used to mold the figure into a fashionable hourglass shape but one that also cramped the organs and made breathing difficult. The corset was worn under a camisole, over which was the blouse or dress, often topped by a scarf. The lower layers of dressing consisted of drawers under a hoop skirt topped with several petticoats and a long skirt that was uncomfortable, unwieldy, or both. Without long, dragging skirts women would have more opportunity for travel and work outside the home. Naturally, many men objected to trousers on women for just this reason, though they had a harder time arguing with the fact that the bloomer costume made household chores easier.

Both Mrs. Stanton and Mrs. Bloomer wore the bloomer costume despite the jeers they drew from men. Although Susan intellectually understood the reason for their attire, she did find it startling at first. In later years, she showed her

support for the costume by wearing it, but she had to overcome her aversion to do so.

Susan and Mrs. Stanton hoped they would work together on some projects and their first chance for a collaboration occurred almost immediately. Mrs. Stanton called a meeting to discuss the founding of a co-educational college that would have the same standards of admission for men and women. Although nothing was to come of this idealistic plan, the meeting was notable for it was there that Susan met Lucy Stone, another woman who had an important influence on Susan's life. It was certainly appropriate for Lucy to be at this meeting because she was one of the first women in the United States to earn a college degree, although she had been discouraged from doing so every step of the way.

Lucy Stone was born in 1818 on a farm in Massachusetts. She lived under the rule of a father who felt that it was decreed by God that men should be dominant over women. Her mother accepted the constant work and subjugation from the head of the household, but Lucy did not. She knew the Bible had been translated by men and decided when she was grown she would learn ancient languages for herself to find out if the translations were accurate. It was a good thing she did not mention this plan to her elders. They would have been happy to inform her how few women, especially on farms, received anything but the most basic education, and she would have learned even more quickly than she did how unsupportive her father could be.

Lucy, a plain, pug-nosed girl, was just into her teens when her father declared that any further education would be

The artist, Nathaniel Currier, satirized
the "Bloomer Costume" in this
picture of a delicate young
woman clad in the fashion
many found outrageous.

wasted on her and that she must leave school. Cleverly, she appealed to his love of thrift by telling him that if she continued, she could get a teaching degree and thus earn money for the family. Reluctantly, Mr. Stone agreed but did not just give her the money for college. He lent it to her and made her sign a note of repayment. After that, she alternately went to school and taught, always trying to earn money for more education. She eventually entered Oberlin College in Ohio, one of the first schools to admit women to a degree program— though college officials gave men preferential treatment and still referred to them as "the leading sex."

Life at college was not easy for Lucy Stone. Women at Oberlin were expected to be quiet, dutiful listeners whose role as students was primarily to prepare themselves to become helpmates and mothers. Lucy, with her ideas about equality of the sexes, was always in trouble with the administration, but after nine years of trying, she finally received her degree at the age of 29. And even after all that time she almost failed to graduate. As an outstanding student, she was required to write an essay to be read at commencement. But as a woman, she was not allowed to read it because public speaking was still considered unseemly for a woman. Moreover, the administration disliked the idea of Lucy even sitting on the platform while a man read the speech because this, too, was considered unladylike. Lucy, who had some notions of making many speeches in the cause of abolition, thought that public-speaking experience was just what she needed and decided she would not write the speech unless she could also read it. The president of Oberlin wanted to make an exception in her case but most of the faculty did not, thinking it would set a bad precedent. The other students sympathized with Lucy and they too refused to submit essays. Finally, there was a kind of compromise. Lucy was not allowed to speak, but she was graduated without writing the essay.

The people's college that Susan Anthony, Lucy Stone and Mrs. Stanton had called the meeting about never got off

Lucy Stone, the early feminist and friend of
Susan B. Anthony, who defied convention in her stand
against the authorities at Oberlin College

the ground, primarily because Horace Greeley, editor of the liberal *New York Tribune*, who they hoped would support them was very hostile to the idea. He felt that co-education would outrage most people. If he supported it, the other reforms that he was interested in might be jeopardized. This was a disappointing experience for Susan, but it served to open her eyes a little further. Susan must now have realized how lucky she was to have a family, and foremost, a father who nurtured her ambitions and supported her goals. And the support was not only emotional. Around this time, Susan decided to become a full-time reform worker, a career that obviously would not pay well, if at all. Daniel urged her to go ahead with her plans and promised her full financial backing.

Susan did not exactly know how she would structure this career, but women's rights was still in third place with her, behind temperance and abolition. For that matter, none of her friends at this time, except perhaps Mrs. Stanton, felt that the women's situation was the primary wrong that needed righting. Lucy Stone was an ardent abolitionist, Amelia Bloomer was devoted to the temperance cause, and Mrs. Stanton kept a strong hand in all the liberal movements of the day. Women's rights in general and women's suffrage in particular were considered things that might be obtained in the distant future. It is fair to say that women reformers cared more about the black man's right to vote than their own.

Then an incident occurred that galvanized Susan's thinking on the issue of women and how they were treated by society. The Sons of Temperance were having a state convention in Albany. Susan and some of the other women delegates were looking forward to being treated as full members in this convention rather than just observers from the women's auxiliaries. But when Susan tried to make a motion, the chairman, shocked that a woman would even think of speaking in a mixed meeting, admonished her: "Sisters were invited here not to speak, but to listen and learn."

An indignant Susan and several of the more courageous

women delegates got up and walked out. On the advice of Lydia Mott, with whom Susan was staying, she hired a room in the Presbyterian church and held a meeting of her own that night. The attendance was not large but it was friendly, and the group decided to form its own state temperance society where women's ideas and speech would be welcome. Susan was quickly appointed chairman of a committee to arrange the first Woman's State Temperance Society convention to be held in Rochester, New York, during the spring of 1852.

Susan then went back to Seneca Falls to discuss with Mrs. Stanton the steps she had taken. Mrs. Stanton could not have been more delighted with these plans, and she promised not only to attend but to make the keynote address. She warned Susan, however, that her speech would be radical, and it was. Most shocking was her declaration that women should be allowed to divorce a man who was drunk. This statement angered the more conservative delegates, to say nothing of the press. Most of the newspapers editorialized against the women for having a convention of their own at all. Still, enough delegates were swayed by Mrs. Stanton's oratory to vote her in as president, a move Susan highly approved. In what was to become a pattern, Susan took the less glamorous job, but the one with more day-to-day responsibilities when she accepted the convention's motion to make her secretary.

A few months later, Susan Anthony's group was invited to attend a Men's State Temperance Society meeting in Syracuse. Susan and Amelia Bloomer were the delegates, but when they arrived, the men jeered them for wearing their bloomer costumes. Susan had just started wearing hers, feeling she could do no less than Mrs. Stanton, Amelia Bloomer, and Lucy Stone, but this was not a very encouraging beginning. One minister on the podium, upon seeing them, burst into a tirade against Susan's temperance society, calling its members "a hybrid species, half man and half woman belonging to neither sex, whose movement must be put down, cut up, branches and roots." Once again the women were not allowed to speak. Susan was appalled, but she was also getting used to this treatment.

The experience did not dissuade her from traveling throughout the state of New York, setting up local chapters of her Woman's State Temperance Society and at the same time gathering petition signatures for a prohibition bill to be introduced in the New York legislature. Luckily, most of her expenses were paid for by an unexpected but logical source—a wealthy soft-drink factory owner who saw great profits ahead for his company if alcohol was to be prohibited.

It was in connection with her efforts for the prohibition bill that Susan began to see how valuable it would be to all the reforms if women had the right to vote. Now all she could do was encourage male legislators to vote a certain way. How much more leverage would women have if they could actually vote the unfriendly legislators out of office!

Though Susan was very involved with her temperance activities, she took time out to attend the third national women's-rights convention held in the fall of 1852. This was Susan's first convention and she missed the presence of Mrs. Stanton, who was home awaiting the birth of her fifth child, but the outstanding list of attendees made up for that disappointment. Among the two thousand delegates were Susan's friend, Lucy Stone, Antoinette Brown, the first ordained woman minister in the United States, Lucretia Mott, and her husband James.

Mrs. Stanton, not able to be there, still managed to make an impact on the convention. She had given Susan a letter to read, and true to form, she included several points that made the delegates take notice. At one point some of them rose from their chairs in a fury. Mrs. Stanton suggested in her letter that it was religion with its teachings of male superiority that had been the greatest detriment to the cause of human rights.

While Elizabeth might have wrestled with this question

in her youth and ended up on the side of liberal dogma, many of the other women reformers (to say nothing of the men) were still quite conservative on religious matters. Mrs. Stanton's questioning of the Bible and indirectly the Almighty, set off a great debate that almost forestalled discussion of all other matters. Susan privately felt that nothing could be decided when it came to religion, but much to her dismay it was a subject that continued to come up.

The press, already firmly against the women's movement, had a field day with this convention. It was derided as a "bloomer convention" and lambasted in the New York editorial pages. As for the clergy, from the pulpit, they denounced the participants as "preachers of such damnable doctrines . . . as would make the demons of the pit shudder to hear."

It is amazing that faced with so much hostility, the advocates of women's rights would persevere, but they strongly believed they were fighting for an idea that someday had to become a reality.

But there were some people, supposedly friends, who were not very happy about Susan and Mrs. Stanton's roles and participation in the women's rights movement. By the time of the second Woman's State Temperance Society convention in June of 1853, both women were being criticized by some society members for not sticking to the temperance issue and always being too ardent in advancing women's rights. Men had always been encouraged to be members of the Woman's State Temperance Society, but Mrs. Stanton and Susan had envisioned this group as one that women would direct and run. Now, the conservative wing of the society gained enough strength to pass an amendment allowing men to become officers. The men took great advantage of this and after Mrs. Stanton lost her bid for re-election as president to a man, a rule was quickly enacted that outlawed any discussion of women's issues at their meetings. Susan and Mrs. Stanton saw their group changing its ways before their very eyes, and they decided to resign.

Mrs. Stanton shrugged off her disappointment by telling Susan that they had more important work to do, bigger fish to fry, but for Susan this was another turning point. She at last clearly saw that a prohibition on liquor would not solve the basic problems of women. They needed to have a stake in their own futures, to be educated, to have control of their own money, and most of all to be able to vote. So Susan and Mrs. Stanton together formulated a new plan. Confident that their strength was in themselves, they were ready for Elizabeth to inspire Susan and for Susan to inspire the nation.

THE PLAN

5

Rather than scattering their energies as they had in the past, Susan Anthony and Mrs. Stanton decided to set some priorities. One goal that at least seemed in reach was an expansion of New York's Women's Property Law of 1848.

The original law had been pushed through the New York legislature primarily by influential men who did not wish to have their daughters' inheritances squandered by greedy or irresponsible husbands. But the law was narrow and only gave a married woman the right to keep in her name property received as a gift or bequeathed to her. While a husband could no longer sell a woman's property without her permission or use it to pay off his debts, this is all it meant. The wife who wanted to sell her own property could not do so because her signature on a contract was not legally valid. On the other hand, if her husband sold the property for her, by law the profits went to him! Nor could a woman's property be left in a will to anyone else without her husband's consent. And the same old laws about a woman's earnings belonging to her husband still applied.

The message that women needed to control their own money was forcefully delivered to Susan during the many days she spent revisiting the towns in which she had set up women's temperance societies the year before. Almost every one of the groups had broken up, mainly because the members had no money of their own for dues, speakers, or any of the other necessities that a club or society would need. Around this time Susan wrote in her diary that she had never really understood just how important financial independence was until she saw that no matter how filled with good intentions a woman's heart was, if she did not have the money or power to act on those intentions, they would not help anyone very much. "Women," she wrote, "must have a purse of their own."

Obviously, the money issue had to be resolved through legislation. But how could women get male legislators to repeal laws that were so obviously to their own sex's benefit? This was the problem that Susan brought to Mrs. Stanton.

Susan had already decided to call yet another convention, this one in the state capital, Albany. The New York legislature would be in session at the same time and Susan wanted Mrs. Stanton to address the joint judiciary committee of the legislature on the matter of women controlling their earnings and property. The United States Constitution gave any citizen the right to petition its governing bodies, and Susan was sure that if anyone could sway the legislators, it would be Mrs. Stanton.

Mrs. Stanton was in favor of the plan, but she was concerned about her role in it. By now she had five little children, and despite her growing prominence, she was more tied down to the house than ever. A speech like the one Susan wanted her to make might be a once-in-a-lifetime opportunity for the feminists and Mrs. Stanton was afraid she did not have the time to do the necessary research. Susan Anthony, however, was not going to allow the strongest speaker in the women's movement to be so burdened with household chores that she could not serve the cause. So she struck a bargain with Mrs. Stanton: Susan and a lawyer friendly to their cause would research all the laws discriminating against women and compile the data if Mrs. Stanton would write and deliver the speech. Mrs. Stanton readily agreed to this, telling Susan she could formulate the speech in her head while she was doing her sewing and baking.

This kind of teamwork set the precedent for the way the two women would work for years to come. Though Susan had a clear, well-modulated speaking voice, she was not very confident about appearing before an audience. Mrs. Stanton, with her penchant for debate, was far more skilled at public speaking, so Susan left that job to her. Likewise, Susan did not think much of her own writing abilities but greatly admired Mrs. Stanton's. In both cases Susan seemed to underestimate her own abilities, but she did take pride in her organizational skills, and along with researching the speech, she took on the arduous task of collecting signatures for petitions that would be presented to the legislature at the same time Mrs. Stanton made her speech.

As Mrs. Stanton wrote in her reminiscences, she was always happy when she and Susan cooperated on a project. They seemed to think as one person and she was delighted by the way they worked together. After many years she wrote: "I am the better writer, she the better critic. She supplied the facts and statistics, I the philosophy and rhetoric and together we have made arguments that have stood unshaken through the storms."

Susan was also the person who prodded Mrs. Stanton when she was not producing as much as Susan thought her fine mind capable. To stimulate her friend's creativity, Susan continually wrote her letters with questions that demanded answers or requested speeches that needed to be written. Mrs. Stanton would try to comply, but sometimes she was so burdened with household obligations that Susan would have to actually visit the Stantons and insist that Mrs. Stanton buckle down while she took over running the Stanton home and minding the children. "Aunt Susan" became quite a favorite with these children although she was much more strict with them than their mother. One of the grown Stanton

children later recalled that while he remembered quite clearly the two women scribbling away, he had no idea at the time they were engaged in anything important.

During the winter of 1853–54, Susan began to think about how she would collect all the signatures she would need for property-law petitions. She finally selected sixty women and assigned each one of them a county in New York to canvass. Susan took the Rochester area and she spent most of that cold, snowy winter tramping from door to door trying to get signatures. The experience was full of revelations for her.

Her heart was touched by the many people who not only signed her petitions, but gave her the hospitality of their tables and their homes. On the other hand, she became even more convinced of the justice of her cause when she saw situations such as that of the young mother who made Susan's supper, prepared her room, washed the dishes, got up early to make breakfast, and then, after Susan paid her for her trouble, had the money taken out of her hand by her husband.

Even harder for Susan to understand were the women who, when asked for their signatures, told Susan they had all the rights they wanted and slammed the door in her face. Other women sarcastically said that unlike Susan they had husbands to take care of them so they did not have to worry about the issues the petitions addressed.

Another trial for Susan during this period was her dedication to the bloomer outfit. She had come to agree with Mrs. Stanton and Lucy Stone that, for psychological reasons, it was important that she wear trousers. And it certainly made

Susan B. Anthony and
Elizabeth Cady Stanton
worked side by side, giving
voice and inspiration to the
struggle for women's rights.

more sense for practical reasons. After all, she spent her days canvassing houses in bone-chilling weather and her nights in drafty taverns or homes that were so cold she needed an ice pick to break the water in her washbowl. The trousers were also easier to walk in than long skirts. The reasonableness of this, however, did not make it any easier for Susan to deal with the hoots and jeers she got when the small-town residents would see her in such outlandish attire. Little boys would follow her down the street convulsed with laughter, while men would lounge in their doorways and snicker, "Here comes my bloomer" as she strode by.

While her personal embarrassment did not keep her from finishing her canvassing, she did vow that after Mrs. Stanton's speech and the Albany convention she would take off the costume for good. Lucy Stone was also mortified by the abuse she got when she wore the bloomer outfit and within the next few years most feminists gave it up. Trousers on women was an idea ahead of its time, but every girl or woman of today who knows the comfort of jeans or slacks must be grateful to these women for first having the courage to wear pants.

By the time Mrs. Stanton finished writing her speech, Susan Anthony and her workers had amassed about six thousand signatures on petitions that called for property and wage reform. Four thousand people had also signed the petition that supported women's suffrage. An impressed legislature set a date in February for the presentation of the petitions and Mrs. Stanton's speech that coincided with the Albany convention.

Mrs. Stanton was uncharacteristically nervous about the speech, so Susan suggested that she submit it to a mutual friend for a critique.

He commended her and Mrs. Stanton felt reassured, but she became agitated all over again when her father called her home to read him the speech.

It was Judge Cady who had told his little daughter that if she did not like certain laws she could petition the legislature to change them. Now that she was about to do just that, he was terribly upset. Actually, father and daughter had been estranged for some time. The Judge grew progressively more horrified each time her views on women's rights, divorce, and religion became known. By this time they were obviously not on very good terms because Judge Cady first heard about her speech from newspaper reports.

Despite their troubles, Mrs. Stanton cared very much about her father's opinion, and on her way to Albany, she stopped in Johnstown to read him her speech. Sitting across from him in his office, Elizabeth Stanton felt embarrassed before her audience of one. Nevertheless, she read the speech aloud and put every bit of emotion—including pathos—she could into it.

To her immense satisfaction, when she finished she saw tears in her father's eyes. Wonderingly, he asked her how a woman who had had such a happy life could know about such things and how she could feel them so intensely. She replied that her emotions had first been touched by the women who came to Judge Cady for help while she listened outside the very office in which they were now sitting.

The judge never actually stated that he supported his daughter's stand on women's rights, but he did offer to help her prepare or check over any future speeches. If she was going to continue making public addresses that contained facts and figures, at least he could see that they were accurate.

Susan Anthony, in her usual efficient manner, had printed twenty thousand copies of Mrs. Stanton's speech and saw that one was placed on the desk of every state senate and assembly member. The speech itself was filled with good, solid examples of how women were discriminated against, and rather than offering vague generalities, Mrs. Stanton gave specific examples of the ways the law could be changed to stamp out the inequities. She told the legislators that even if they could do nothing more than follow the Golden Rule, that in itself would be a large step toward giving women freedom from oppression.

Although there were the usual detractors, Mrs. Stanton's speech and the petitions impressed a number of the lawmakers. While these male legislators did not seem inclined to change the laws, for the first time they admitted there were injustices. The former governor of New York told Mrs. Stanton that while she had reason on her side, custom and prejudice were against her and "they are stronger than truth and logic."

Mrs. Stanton, of course, received the lion's share of attention because she was the person who had given the speech, but those in the women's movement were well aware of the part Susan had played. Lucy Stone wrote to her and blessed her for her courage in continuing even in the face of discouragement. She also told her that her example of positive action was just the sort of thing women needed to see.

Discouragement was certainly what followed. Despite the positive response to Mrs. Stanton's speech, the matter was referred to a legislative committee where it died. This did not deter Susan Anthony. She once again organized a group to collect even more signatures and soon she was canvassing again.

Susan's trips were extremely well planned. She sent out advance notices of her arrival and wrote to local officials asking them to put up posters or place advertisements in the newspaper about the speeches she was now giving in addition to her canvassing. Her routing was the same everywhere. She would allow a day for travel, and after what was often a difficult trip, she would arrive in the morning at the town where a speech or meeting had been arranged. In the afternoon, she would give half of her speech, after which she would get signatures for her ever-growing petitions and sell pamphlets to raise money for her expenses. In the evening, she charged a small fee to hear the rest of this speech, and in general she drew good crowds, though many people probably came just for the novelty of listening to a woman speak.

In some of the places to which Susan traveled she was well known, and one of these was Canajoharie where she had been the headmistress at the academy. She was not sure how she would be received and she was grateful when her uncle, Joshua Read, helped once more by arranging for her to use the Methodist church for her speech. Susan had nothing to worry about. She was welcomed back warmly; in fact the town residents were so happy to see her, they asked her to return to her old teaching position there. This Uncle Joshua protested vehemently, saying that many people could teach but only Susan could do her present job.

As she continued on her self-imposed lecture circuit during December of 1854, Susan was encouraged by the fact that at last she was getting some favorable news coverage and even in hostile communities there was usually someone who would offer her a meeting place or lodgings. Oddly, men seemed more swayed by her views than women. The women's rights groups she tried to set up in each town were usually headed by women who took on the job because their husbands had urged them to.

After eight long months on the road, Susan returned home to the farm in May of 1855. Her accomplishments of that period were duly noted in her diary. She had been to fifty-four counties, sold twenty thousand pamphlets, and after paying her expenses showed a net profit of seventy dollars which she immediately put toward the next campaign.

That summer, despite her success, Susan felt fatigued and unwell—a rare condition for her. Perhaps it was because of the grueling physical hardships she had undergone while traveling during freezing weather; in any case, she was exhausted and complained of arthritic pains throughout her body.

She also felt psychologically defeated. Susan was very upset by the news that Lucy Stone and Antoinette Brown had married the Blackwell brothers, Henry and Samuel, themselves members of a remarkable family of reformers that included their sister Elizabeth, America's first female physician.

Lucy Stone had planned to remain unmarried and

though she was attracted to Henry Blackwell, she intensely disliked the institution of marriage and what women gave up for it. Henry was a persistent suitor, however, and after numerous assurances that he agreed with her strong feminist views, Lucy consented to marry the young man who was seven years her junior.

But even after Henry publicly stated he would give up all the rights and privileges normally given to a husband, there was one problem that still remained. More than a century before the present trend, Lucy Stone decided that she wanted to keep her own name. As far as she was concerned, Lucy felt no kinship to the name Blackwell and to be addressed as Mrs. Blackwell, she thought, was to lose her own identity. The ever sympathetic Henry understood her feelings about this issue and told Lucy he had no problem with her retaining the name Stone, but she realized that even with Henry's support, it would be a daring step. It was, but by keeping her own name, she also conferred it upon the small number of women of her era who followed her example. They became collectively known as "Lucy Stoners." It was not until the 1970s, however, that women retained their names in any great numbers. Ironically, more than 130 years after Lucy Stone's decision, women who keep their maiden names still face some of the same legal problems and embarrassing social situations that she had to endure.

While Susan Anthony showed a glimmer of happiness about Lucy's bold decision concerning her name, she was decidedly unhappy about the Blackwell marriages. Uncharacteristically, she saw the issue only from her own point of view—Lucy Stone and Antoinette Brown, two of her staunchest and most reliable coworkers, would now be busy taking care of husbands and starting families. Shades of Elizabeth Cady Stanton, Susan must have thought! She even wrote to Mrs. Stanton lamenting this turn of events, saying that it was a crime that three such talented women should turn themselves over to "baby-making."

So, feeling defeated on several fronts, Susan decided to

go to a spa run by her cousin Seth in Worcester, Massachusetts, to take the water cure, a treatment that involved drinking lots of mineral water and taking plenty of relaxing baths. By winter, when it was once more time to continue on the speaking circuit, Susan was feeling much better. Instead of traveling alone, she hired a noted reformer and author of children's books, Frances D. Gage, to share the platform with her. The well-known Mrs. Gage drew good crowds, to Susan's intense pleasure. And in weather that was even harsher than the winter before, Susan had a companion during the long waits for trains or while traveling in open sleighs to towns where the trains did not run.

After two arduous years of work, Susan went once more to Albany when the legislature was in session and again presented her petitions. Hopeful because the response the previous time had been encouraging if not affirmative, Susan was severely disappointed when the judiciary committee not only ignored her proposal, they made a joke out of it. Women, they said, always got the best seats, the choicest bits of food, and in general were put on a pedestal. If anyone had a right to complain, they laughed, it was the men.

Legislators who thought that their sarcasm would deter Susan Anthony did not know her. Their rebuff merely galvanized her to greater action. She was comforted by the fact that even if the New York lawmakers were lagging with the times, other people were not. Lucy Stone, writing from Ohio where she was now living, reported that her state had passed a liberal women's property law. England, too, was moving ahead on this issue. Just as welcome was the news that some substantial funds were finally coming into the movement. In 1858, Wendell Phillips, a reformer and friend of Garrison, told Susan that an anonymous gentleman had donated $5,000 for the women's movement. He, Lucy Stone, and Susan had been named the trustees. The next year philanthropist Charles F. Hovey left an estate of $50,000, which he willed to several reform movements, women's rights among them.

Joyously, Susan took fifteen hundred dollars of the money and spent it for speakers, conventions, pamphlets, and publicity. She continued to bombard the New York legislature with petitions, and at long last, in 1860, success seemed imminent. Susan was told by a friendly legislator that if she could get Mrs. Stanton to speak for the bill one more time, it would probably pass. Once more Susan hurried to Seneca Falls to care for the Stanton household while Mrs. Stanton prepared her speech.

With Susan watching from the gallery, Mrs. Stanton spoke before a joint session of the legislature in March of 1860. This time the men were ready to act and the next day they passed The Married Women's Property Bill. Now it was legal in New York for a married woman to have sole responsibility for her property and earnings. She could sue in court and she also had the right to obtain joint custody of her children. It had taken seven long, hard years, but one of the first significant steps in the journey toward women's rights had been taken.

THE
WAR YEARS

6

For most people living in the United States in 1860, the news of the New York Women's Property Law, if they heard about it at all, paled in comparison to the war talk that was swirling all around them. During the 1850s, there was almost continuous quarreling between the Northern, Southern, and Western sections of the country. Besides arguing about different kinds of legislation that was being passed, they also held different views on how strong the national government should be. The South resisted measures that would strengthen the federal government; it wanted mainly to be left alone.

Mixed up with these sectional demands was the slavery issue. Some people fought to keep slavery out of the new territories, others insisted it be allowed, and still others were for compromise. The abolitionists, who wanted to destroy slavery everywhere, were only a small minority, but through speeches, pamphlets, articles, books such as *Uncle Tom's Cabin,* and direct measures such as the underground railway, they continued to remind people that slavery was wrong. In the end, it was many reasons, not just one, that started the Civil War.

During the years before the Civil War, Susan had been immersed in women's rights work, but that had not stopped her from doing her part for the abolitionists at the same time. In 1855 she had received an offer from the Anti-slavery Society to act as its emissary in New York. Susan thought hard about whether she could handle another job but she finally accepted, feeling that the slavery issue needed all the dedicated workers it could find. Her job was very much the same as the one she was performing for women's rights. She arranged speaking tours and meetings and had posters printed and displayed. If the main speakers could not appear, she spoke herself.

Susan's personal heroes at this time were abolitionist and journalist William Lloyd Garrison and Wendell Phillips, another abolitionist and reformer, whose motto was "no Union with slave holders." They were in the most radical fringe of the abolition movement. Their group even disliked Lincoln and the Republicans, feeling that they stood for accommodation and compromise. While much of the country recoiled at the thought that the Southern states might secede from the Union, these abolitionists were not terribly bothered. They thought that having the Southern states form their own country would prevent the curse of slavery from spreading to the Western territories.

Susan's family also continued to be deeply involved in the abolition movement. Her youngest brother, Merritt, living in Kansas, was among those fighting the proslavery agitators with radical abolitionist John Brown. Her father's house became another Rochester stop on the underground railway, and despite the danger, the Anthonys helped slaves flee to freedom in Canada.

In March of 1857 the Supreme Court handed down a decision in the Dred Scott case. This was a complicated matter involving Scott, a slave, who was suing for his freedom after having been moved to Illinois and the Wisconsin territory, areas where slavery was prohibited. Scott lost the case, and the Court's ruling, among other things, said the Constitution did not protect blacks because they had not been citizens when the document was adopted.

The decision made an indignant Susan throw herself even more fully into the abolition cause. Formerly nervous on the speaking platform, this new blow to the antislavery movement angered Susan so much that she put away her prepared speeches and began to speak from her heart. Because she did not write down her thoughts, few speeches from this period exist, but one that does contains such crowd-stirring phrases as "the bloated self-conceit of traitors and rebels" and "the hydra-monster which sucks its life blood from the unpaid, unpitied toll of slaves." Her rhetoric in the cause of women's rights rarely reached such passionate heights, and in some ways, Susan in this period of her life seemed to have been more emotionally invested in abolition than in any other cause. Even years after the war was over, Susan found it difficult to have generous feelings toward the South.

The scorn that Susan received for her women's rights work was nothing compared to what she and other abolitionists faced from Northerners who thought they were troublemakers who intended to destroy the Union.

If Susan's speeches became more dynamic, it was because the times demanded it. She and other antislavery speakers combed New York towns looking for support; mobs disrupted their gatherings, rioters locked them out of their halls, and when they did have an audience, some of its members carried weapons while others threw rotten eggs. In one especially frightening episode in Syracuse, Susan and another speaker were burned in effigy. In Albany, only the sight of the mayor sitting grimly with a rifle across his knees prevented the mob from storming the meeting.

Ironically, just at the moment when Susan was doing the most to keep the abolition movement going, she was also antagonizing the two most powerful men in the abolition (and women's) movement, her mentors, William Lloyd Garrison and Wendell Phillips.

The division started over the troublesome issue of

divorce. Divorce laws in the United States were very strict and very much in favor of husbands. Almost always, it was the wife who was censured and left with nothing after a divorce. Her husband could be a drunkard, a scoundrel, or worse, but still he was entitled to his children, and in most states, to his former wife's earnings!

Many people of the era, including reformers, literally believed that marriages were made in heaven and that they should not be dissolved no matter what the circumstances. Mrs. Stanton thought this view was nonsense and decided to bring up the issue at the next women's convention. She did so in the form of a resolution which urged members to advocate divorce in cases where one or both parties did not feel they could continue the marriage. Though Susan did not know Mrs. Stanton was going to introduce this resolution, she totally agreed with her friend's views and supported the motion; she was surprised when Phillips demanded that the resolution be removed from the record because it had no relevancy to the convention. Garrison agreed with Phillips on the relevancy issue, though he did not feel the resolution needed to be stricken. Susan quickly got to her feet to tell the men and the rest of the audience that marriage had always been a one-sided matter with men gaining everything and women losing everything. If any issue belonged in a discussion of women's rights, marriage and divorce certainly did, and if Messrs. Garrison and Phillips could not see that it was too bad. The resolution was eventually tabled, though not stricken from the record, a solution that satisfied no one. There were hard feelings all around, and for the first time, but not the last, Susan wondered if she was putting her faith in the wrong men.

Soon after this incident, Susan took another stand that displeased Garrison and Phillips, but one to which Susan felt committed. Mrs. Abner Phelps, the wife of a Massachusetts state senator, Dr. Phelps, and the mother of his children, found out that her husband was involved with another woman. But when she confronted him with the evidence, he replied that she was insane, convinced a doctor this was so, and had her committed to a mental institution. Eventually, Mrs. Phelps's brother obtained her release, but when she was free, the woman was in despair when she learned that, according to Massachusetts law, her husband would obtain custody of their children. She turned to Lydia Mott for help and it was at Miss Mott's house that she met Susan Anthony. Susan decided this woman, like the runaway slaves of the underground railway, needed someone to help her to freedom and that she would be that person.

Mrs. Phelps's daughter was with her, and rather than risk everything by trying to take all three of her children, Susan realized it would be better just to try to get mother and daughter to New York City. Susan, Mrs. Phelps, and her daughter boarded a train, the escapees in disguise. In New York, Susan tried to get a hotel room, but no one would take them because they were not escorted by a man. Finally, it was so late that Susan threatened to stay in a lobby all night if her party was not given a room; the clerk gave them a tiny room with no fire. The next day they again searched for lodgings. At last, a woman reformer took them in after a number of refusals by other people who Susan thought would help. It was not long before Dr. Phelps realized who had probably helped his wife and child escape. Susan was bombarded with letters and telegrams demanding to know their whereabouts, but in her practical way Susan just ignored them. The letters were not only from Phelps and his family but from reformers who felt Susan should not keep a child from her father's control. The letter that rankled the most, however, came from Garrison and Phillips, who wrote her that having one of their abolition workers under suspicion cast a pall over the whole movement. They argued that since the laws in Massachusetts gave child-custody rights to the father, Susan should abide by those laws. This reasoning was almost laughable to Susan because, as she pointed out to Garrison, he broke the law every time he helped a slave escape.

The deeper issue was that Garrison and Phillips failed to see that a woman could be in bondage to her husband even as a slave was to his master. In essence, this is why they could not accept the idea of changing the divorce laws either. Susan thought it incredible that men who could be so clear on one issue of injustice could be so muddled on a parallel matter involving women.

By early 1861 seven states had seceded from the Union. Despite the turmoil in the country, Susan wanted to call the yearly women's rights convention. The only year that had been missed until now was 1856 when, to Susan's dismay, the convention had to be cancelled because all the best speakers were pregnant. Other than that occasion, the convention had been an annual event for a decade. But now no one seemed interested, and even Mrs. Stanton felt that the country was in such a devastating state that women's concerns must take a back seat for a while. Susan disagreed. She also felt that the feminists who said that the women's contributions to the war effort would be rewarded by the vote were being unrealistic.

Many women were involved in helping the North. By the time the war was officially underway in 1861, manpower was in short supply and women had to fill the void. Thousands of ordinary women took over farms and businesses while their men were away fighting. The women's movement had long urged women to get involved in these kinds of everyday pursuits, but for most, it was the necessity of war that made them do it. Some women became quite prominent at this time. Reformer Dorothea Dix was the Superintendent of Nurses for the Union and sent three thousand women into the field. Dr. Elizabeth Blackwell helped recruit nurses as did Clara Barton, who later founded the American Red Cross.

Oddly, Susan Anthony, along with many other women who were active in the feminist movement, did not take much part in the war work at first. One reason Susan did not join in immediately was her commitment to total emancipation of the slaves. The war was not being fought to free the slaves, it was being fought to preserve the Union. Susan would have been content to have the South form its own union, and therefore did not really support the war. Besides, with her pacifist Quaker background, she abhorred war on general principles. Thus, the spring of 1861 found Susan sitting at home on the farm in Rochester with time on her hands.

The country's loss of Susan's services was the family's gain. She decided to take over the farm work for a while, allowing Daniel to take a long-desired trip to Kansas to see his sons. This visit also gave Susan the chance to spend some time with her mother and her sister, Mary.

When Daniel returned home, Susan abandoned her planting, canning, quilting, and other chores to make a lecture tour for the Anti-slavery Society. She also took some time in 1862 to help Mrs. Stanton move her family from Seneca Falls to Brooklyn, New York, where Henry Stanton had found a new job as a newspaper reporter. It was around this time that the shocked women learned that while the country had been absorbed with the war, the New York legislature had amended the 1860 Married Women's Property Law for which feminists had worked so long and hard. The legislators removed the equal-guardianship-of-children clause as well as the one that gave widows control over their own property.

This outrage made Susan feel even more deeply that women should not sit back and lose their advantages while the war went on. She tried to gain support for another convention, but women did not rally to her call. This left Susan frustrated yet determined to somehow continue the fight.

A more personal blow also struck Susan in 1862. After a brief illness, her father, Daniel Anthony, died at his home; he was sixty-eight. Daniel had helped Susan in innumerable ways, both financially and emotionally. He was the high standard by which she would continue to judge all men, just as her friend Mrs. Stanton was her standard for women. Though grieved, Susan was grateful that she had been able to benefit from his love and support for forty-two years of her life. He had never failed her.

A bereaved Susan now desperately needed something important to do and turned once more to Mrs. Stanton for inspiration. Mrs. Stanton, who was also restless, had been thinking about the war. She felt that too many women thought only in terms of practical work to help the effort. Perhaps there could be some intellectual outlet for women who wanted to affect the policies of the country. Susan and Mrs. Stanton, after much discussion, decided to form the Women's National Loyal League. One of the League's goals was to see that the newly issued Emancipation Proclamation, which freed the slaves in the Confederate states, would be expanded into a Thirteenth Amendment to the Constitution that would abolish slavery throughout the land. If Mrs. Stanton once more provided the rhetoric, Susan was sure she could get thousands of signed petitions to present to Congress.

The first meeting of the Women's National Loyal League was held in May of 1863 in New York. Susan presided and the meeting was filled with old, familiar reformers ready to show the nation that women were useful for more than rolling bandages.

Matters, as usual, did not run completely smoothly. Susan proposed a resolution stating that a true peace could not be established until blacks and women had obtained their civil rights. Immediately, a cry arose from a group in the audience that the slavery issue should not be linked with women's rights, but the feminists prevailed.

Mrs. Stanton was elected president of the group and Susan was named secretary. The first act of the League was to send a letter of appreciation to President Lincoln commending him on the Emancipation Proclamation and thanking him especially for the freedom of black women. They also informed him that the league was going to petition Congress for a Thirteenth Amendment that would abolish slavery forever in the United States.

The next move was to begin a massive petition undertaking that would obtain a million signatures. Susan rented a bare little room at the Cooper Institute and from this humble office she geared herself to the task of having petitions printed, sent to canvassers, and sorted when they were returned. She received a salary of twelve dollars a week, the least amount, she figured, with which she could make do. Despite her low wages, the project was still woefully short of funds. Then Susan had an idea. She would charge each person who signed the petition a penny for the privilege. This ploy garnered the movement three thousand dollars.

For the first time in her life Susan did not have Daniel Anthony's financial aid to fall back on, and she experienced at first hand what life was like for a woman living alone in New York. Henry Stanton had changed jobs once more. Now he was working at the *New York Tribune*, and the Stanton family was living in Manhattan after their brief stay in Brooklyn. The Stantons allowed Susan to rent a room with them for a modest sum, which helped her budget. She wrote home that she economized at lunch by eating the same thing every day— berries, tea rusks, and milk. Another money-saving measure was walking to work each day even though the distance between the Stanton's house and Susan's office was considerable.

There was one period where this long walk was also dangerous. During the spring of 1863, a new draft law was about to go into effect, and poor Northern men were irate that the rich could pay other men as substitutes to fulfill their draft obligations while those with less money had no other choice than to be drafted. The focus of their anger was directed at blacks and abolitionists, and eventually rioting broke out. The mobs rampaged for more than a week, and hundreds of blacks were killed.

The well-known abolitionists were also at risk, and Mrs. Stanton had a plan for escaping her home through the skylights and across the roof to a neighbor's house if rioters should storm her house. Fortunately, it never came to that, but the danger was very real. Only a few blocks away, the Colored Orphans' Asylum was burned to the ground. Despite the dangers, Susan continued trying to get to her office during the long, hot summer of 1863.

Susan's efforts began to pay off in February of 1864 when she presented to a friendly legislator, Senator Sumner of Massachusetts, the first installment of 100,000 signatures, which he agreed to introduce in the Congress. A few months later she sent him more petitions containing another 300,000 signatures. The Thirteenth Amendment, which outlawed slavery, was introduced in Congress on February 1, 1865, passed state ratification by December, and became a part of the Constitution. Its speedy passage was due, in part, to its strong public support.

Once the Amendment was ratified, the work of the Women's Loyal League was finished. It was time for Susan to vacate her office at the institute and close the books. Through private donations and her penny-a-signature policy, Susan raised almost the entire financing. There remained only a debt of $4.72, which she paid herself.

As soon as the war ended, the battle for black suffrage began. The Thirteenth Amendment, which was in the process of being ratified by the states, only freed the slaves. New legislation would be needed to give blacks full citizenship, which, of course, included the right to vote. Now a crucial split appeared among the reformers. The leaders of the women's movement were ready to press forward with their own demands for suffrage. They actually did not think that women's suffrage would be difficult to secure. As had been predicted, the women of the Union had been invaluable to the war effort. They had proven they had leadership abilities, intelligence, and business sense. There certainly seemed no reason why they should not become full citizens of the country which they had just worked so hard to preserve.

Therefore, it was a rude shock when the feminists learned that the cause of women's suffrage was being thwarted by the very men who had once been their champions—Garrison, Phillips, and Horace Greeley. The men argued that mixing the black and women's suffrage movements would be a mistake. Blacks might lose more support than women would gain. Susan was furious—not only had women worked long and hard for this right, but in most cases they were better educated and had more political experience than the freed slaves. Mrs. Stanton saw more practical problems. The initial draft of the Fourteenth Amendment used the word "male" for the first time in the Constitution. If the amendment was drafted in this form, it would take another amendment to get women the vote, and pushing through a second suffrage amendment could take years. Susan and Mrs. Stanton decided that they had better get the women's movement moving again before it was too late.

They immediately produced ten thousand signatures on petitions for Congress, but suddenly their old friends in Washington who had been happy to introduce antislavery petitions now became uncooperative. Senator Sumner, a Republican, told them this was an inopportune moment for women to ask for voting rights. What he meant was, that since the Republicans were the party that backed emancipation, if black men got the vote they would probably all become Republicans. This was what the Senator and his fellow party members badly wanted. On the other hand, they thought women would probably vote as their husbands did, and while some women would be Republicans, there was no point in enfranchising many potential Democrats as well. When Susan saw that no help would be coming from her former backers, she turned to any maverick Congressmen who might help her present her petitions.

Susan and Mrs. Stanton's next move was to call a women's rights convention in the spring of 1866. Susan hoped to form an American Equal Rights Association which would work for both black and woman suffrage. She felt the equal-rights group should incorporate Garrison's Anti-slavery Society since the two groups would be duplicating their work. The groups did merge, but it was not long before the pro-black suffrage segment gained ascendency with the cry, "This is the Negro's hour." When Susan and Mrs. Stanton realized that their male supporters (and even a portion of the women) were for women's suffrage only intellectually and

Elizabeth Cady Stanton addressed a meeting
of the Senate Committee considering the right
of women to vote, but the petition for
a constitutional amendment found little
sympathy in Washington in the 1860s.

would not offer any practical help, they disgustedly decided to devote themselves to the woman's cause alone.

Sojourner Truth, a former slave, abolitionist, and feminist, told a meeting of the Equal Rights Association that if only black men received the vote, black women would be doubly oppressed, but even this did not impress the members. Once more the ardent feminists began to hear the tired, old arguments that women did not really need the right to vote since they ruled the world with a glance of their eye. This remark came from their "friend" Horace Greeley.

Since each state would have a say in deciding who among U.S. residents could vote, Susan and Mrs. Stanton decided to embark on speaking tours in New York and Kansas, where the matter was being discussed. In spite of their efforts in New York, when that state drew up its new Constitution, it provided for black male suffrage alone.

Disappointed, Susan and Mrs. Stanton moved on to Kansas, where the question of black and female suffrage was being put to the people directly in a referendum. This proved to be an arduous trip notable for bad food, difficult travel, bedbugs in their accommodations, and prejudice against their cause. To make things even worse for Susan, her reputation as troublemaker had preceded her, but Mrs. Stanton, the image of motherliness, was at times able to win her audiences over. In the end, all the hardships were for nothing. Kansas voted to enfranchise neither blacks nor women.

This was a difficult period for Susan. Most observers later felt that this was the crucial moment when, with enough pressure, the vote for both groups could have been gained. Instead, the male leadership of the reform movement betrayed their feminist friends and even won many women to their side by telling them that women should be considerate and let the black man have his chance. Even ardent feminists fell prey to this argument. Susan did not, however. Though she believed strongly in black suffrage, she told one male reformer, "I would sooner cut off my right hand than ask for the ballot for the black man and not for woman."

Now, it became abundantly clear that many men—even the most progressive—could not, or would not, understand the humiliation of a woman's position and her need for the vote. If women were to win their rights, they would have to stay their course and not shirk from a fight. What Susan and Mrs. Stanton did not fully realize was that much of the fighting would be within the ranks of their own group.

THE REVOLUTION

7

When Susan decided to devote her life to the struggle for human rights, she knew that she would be spending more time thinking about other people's lives than hers. But as a woman alone she also had to take responsibility for her own well being. As Susan became more prominent, she had to develop a thick skin so she would not be hurt by her detractors' comments.

At the end of the Civil War Susan was forty-five years old and at a crucial point in her personal life. Antifeminist newspapers made fun of her, calling her, among other things, an old sourpuss, and they mocked what they considered to be her spinsterish ways. One detractor, an abolitionist, said Susan had no right to speak about marriage and divorce since she was not married. She retorted that in that case he had no right to speak about slavery because he had never been a slave.

Few people knew that Susan had received more than a fair share of marriage proposals. As late as 1858, when her feminist friends were at home having babies, she wondered whether or not she too should just give in and accept one of her suitors. She wrote Mrs. Stanton: "I have very weak moments and long to lay my weary head somewhere. . . . I sometimes fear that I too shall faint by the wayside and drop out of the ranks of the faithful few."

Indeed, there was one suitor at this time for whom Susan seems to have had a great deal of affection. She did not name him in her diary, but she did write about moonlight rides and called him "marvelously attentive." She also said he was intelligent, but lamented that he did not have much "backbone." Apparently this was enough to keep him from any further serious consideration. Later, in 1863, she received a proposal by mail from an old beau now living in Ohio. His first wife had recently died and since he still cherished fond memories of Susan he asked if she would be interested in resuming their former relationship. But by then Susan was so involved with her war work she politely declined without giving the matter much thought.

Susan's major objection to marriage was that, from her observations, women always got the short end of the bargain. In a lecture she gave before the war titled "The True Woman," Susan stressed that a woman must develop her intellect and talents. Only then could she expect to enter marriage as an equal. She felt that to undertake marriage in any other way was not worth the price that most women seemed inevitably to pay.

After Daniel Anthony's death, Lucy Anthony, now seventy-one, found the farm outside of Rochester too much for her to manage, so she decided to sell it and move to the city with her daughter Mary. Susan knew that selling the farm was the most practical thing to do, but it nevertheless was painful to part with the place that represented tranquility and refuge. Sadly, she helped pack the mementos of over forty years and moved her mother and sister to a red brick house on a lovely, tree-lined street in Rochester. The house had a room for Susan and it was close to the homes of her sisters, Guelma and Hannah, and their families. Susan was glad that they were all in close proximity, and she especially enjoyed spending time with Guelma and Aaron McLean's daughter,

23-year-old Ann Eliza. Suddenly, in 1864, the girl died, and Susan was devastated by the loss.

To raise her spirits, Susan decided to put aside her work for a while and take advantage of a long-standing invitation to visit her brother, Daniel, Jr., and his wife, Anne, who lived in Leavenworth, Kansas. Wearing a new five-dollar silk dress, Susan took the train ticket Daniel sent and headed out West.

Daniel, Jr., had made quite a success of his life in Leavenworth. When he first arrived there, eight years before, the town had eight thousand residents. Now it boasted a population of twenty-two thousand. Daniel not only published a newspaper there, he was the postmaster and the mayor. In fact, he was campaigning for re-election when Susan arrived. After welcoming her, he quickly handed over some of the responsibilities of his newspaper. With the promise of work to do, Susan settled comfortably into her brother's green-shuttered cottage.

Daniel told Susan that he wanted to make his newspaper "radical," but it soon became apparent that brother and sister disagreed on the meaning of that word. Daniel promptly rejected Susan's plan to fill the paper with articles about black suffrage and women's rights. That left Susan the boring task of editing and rewriting the articles that came in from other sources. A break in the monotony came with a visit from her brother Merritt, who was still in the Union army at the time. Merritt had come West years before when he was virtually a boy. Like so many other men, the war had taken his youth and his energy. It must have come as a shock to Susan to see her baby brother now a hardened soldier in his thirties.

Possessing a dynamic nature, Susan did not put up with her boredom very well. She began looking around for something to do other than rewriting newspaper articles and sewing baby clothes for her brother's child. She got a chance to re-enter the fray when she was invited to speak at the traditional Fourth of July festivities. She delivered a rousing speech to an enthusiastic crowd against the reconstruction policies of President Andrew Johnson; as usual she also included a plea for women's rights.

The 1865 visit to Kansas was a mild forerunner to the trip she made in 1867 with Mrs. Stanton. On that important visit, Susan put everything she had into gaining support for the suffrage amendment. Two propositions were offered, and male citizens could vote for either, neither, or both. The first was to remove the word "male" from the voting requirements in the state constitution; the other was to remove the word "white." This was the first time the public was to have its feelings on the matter polled. As mentioned, both of those issues failed to gain passage, but one very significant thing did happen during the canvassing of Kansas—Susan and Mrs. Stanton met George Francis Train for the first time.

Train was sent to Kansas by the St. Louis Suffrage Association. The association had asked Susan and Mrs. Stanton if they wanted some help, and the two thought they could use an extra speaker or two on the platform. But when Train appeared, the women found themselves in a quandary. Train was a Democrat, and while they realized he could probably help stir Kansas Democrats to their cause, they had never really worked with anyone from that party. As far as they and all their fellow reformers were concerned, the Democrats were the party of the slaveholders and in general were anathema to the Republicans and the abolitionists. Mrs. Stanton and Susan knew that by accepting Train's help they would be alienating many of their friends back East. On the other hand, friends such as Garrison certainly had not been very helpful lately, so they decided to take aid where they found it.

Train had other problems besides his party affiliation. An Easterner by birth, and Irish by ancestry, Train was a flamboyant financier and the picture of sartorial splendor. He was an urbane, witty man who held all sorts of controversial views. He was for a lowered, eight-hour working day, he thought government bills should be paid with paper dollars (or greenbacks) instead of gold, and he held strong pro-union feelings. Oddly, black suffrage was not very high on his list of priorities, and it was this that most aroused the disapproval of the abolitionists.

Considering Train's nonchalance about the blacks' plight, it is difficult to understand how Susan could associate herself with him. The answer lies with the Republicans and reformers she thought were on her side. From the time she and Mrs. Stanton arrived in Kansas these groups had waged open warfare against them. Even some blacks—former friends—were traveling around the state asking that women be denied the same voting privileges they were asking for themselves. This was a bitter pill to swallow, and it made George Train's involvement with their cause more palatable.

It was not long before he won over Susan and Mrs. Stanton completely. In a move that greatly impressed the women, he willingly accepted the financial burden for his speaking tour. At a time when every penny counted (and there were few pennies to count), this was a real boon. He delivered rousing speeches and was very effective in getting the Democrats in the audience, especially Irish railroad workers, to support the women's cause. Train himself, in his mid-thirties, was a handsome man with a head full of curls, penetrating dark eyes, and a captivating manner. On the speaking platform he was something to behold.

Initially, Train was supposed to tour the state with another local Democrat, but when this man dropped out, Train at first said the route was too difficult for any man and that he did not want to travel alone. Susan suggested she travel with him instead, and he agreed.

What a pair they must have made—Susan, a simply dressed, quietly groomed middle-aged woman taking all things in her stride, and Train, the effervescent Beau Brummell, always concerned that he should have a bath and fresh linen before every speech. Strange as it may seem, this odd couple got along famously.

They traveled all through Kansas together, speaking in front of audiences large and small. Train was able to captivate even hostile audiences with his wit. His favorite line, thundered at the end of each speech, was: "Every man in Kansas who throws a vote for the Negro and not the women has insulted his mother; his daughter, his sister, and his wife."

Train's techniques were effective and even though the women's suffrage proposal was not ratified in Kansas, both Susan and Mrs. Stanton felt that Train was in part responsible for the sizable vote they did roll up.

One day while they were traveling through Kansas, Train asked Susan why there was no feminist newspaper. When she informed him it was from lack of money, but not ability, he offered to finance a paper in exchange for a column of his own and some space for his financial opinions. Susan had long wanted to start a newspaper that could be a clearinghouse for women's matters, but the always precarious financial situation of the movement had made this a pipe dream. Now here was a man casually offering to make her dream a reality.

At first Susan thought perhaps Train was speaking off the top of his expensive hat, but at the very next whistle stop, he told the audience to watch for the new feminist newspaper whose motto would be: "Men, their rights and nothing more; women, their rights and nothing less." Slowly, Susan began to realize Train was serious about his offer.

After the Kansas trip was over, Train had another proposition for Susan and Mrs. Stanton. Instead of rushing back to New York, he would finance a leisurely speaking tour for all of them. They would go to Chicago, Cleveland, Cincinnati, and other big cities where the citizens had never had the opportunity to hear the famous suffrage duo of Susan Anthony and Mrs. Stanton.

After traveling in open buckboard carriages on bumpy roads through wild country for months, the women were certainly tempted by the chance to visit the nation's cities in style. But more important, they did not want to pass up the chance to spread the feminist doctrine among the uninitiated. Train was not simply being generous in paying for this trip; there were several advantages in it for him. For one thing, Mrs. Stanton's famous name and reputation for oratory would surely draw a crowd. This huge audience would also have to listen to him talk about his favorite subjects because he would be sharing the platform. Train also knew from first-hand experience that if Susan made the travel arrangements, he would have a far better tour than he could have organized by himself.

By the time this successful lecture tour was underway, Susan and Mrs. Stanton had heard from many of their former supporters, and opinion was vehemently against Train and their alliance with him. William Lloyd Garrison and Wendell Phillips were particularly upset. It was difficult for the women to separate themselves from their old friends, but they knew from sad experience that most reformers would not support women's suffrage at this time whether Susan and Mrs. Stanton were affiliated with Train or not. So, for practical reasons, since the women were determined to wage the fight for the vote, they decided to do so with the help of Train's money.

Once they were back in New York, Train immediately made good on his promise to finance a women's newspaper. Within a month after their return, the first issue of *The Revolution* was selling on the newsstands on January 8, 1869; Mrs. Stanton and Parker Pillsbury, a reformer and journalist for the *Anti-slavery Standard*, were the editors. Susan's name appeared on the masthead as the managing editor. The name *Revolution* probably came from Mrs. Stanton's feelings that the Civil War and its upheavals were a second revolution for the United States. It proved to be an apt name for a paper that generated some upheavals all its own.

The Revolution was welcomed by a few of its competitors but ignored by most of them. Whatever their feelings about the paper's content, all agreed it was an especially handsome-looking sixteen-page newspaper with large clear type and an orderly layout.

Susan was delighted with the result of their hard work and gave much of the credit to George Train's enthusiasm for the project. Therefore, she was dismayed to learn that Train planned to leave America for a while. As soon as the first issue appeared, Train sailed for England where he was going to campaign for another of his controversial causes, freedom for Ireland. True to his word, he left six hundred dollars to be used for the publication of *The Revolution* in his absence, with the promise of more upon his return. Unfortunately, when he arrived in England he was promptly arrested for his Irish sympathies, spending the next months in a British jail. Susan quickly realized that Train's money would not last very long and that once again the financial responsibility for the women's project would fall on her shoulders. She knew also that raising money would not be easy, considering the controversial content of the newspaper.

Susan, Mrs. Stanton, and Parker Pillsbury wanted *The Revolution* to venture far beyond the issue of suffrage and even beyond the general topic of women's rights. Anything that even touched upon the concerns of women would appear in their newspaper. There were articles about education, job training, women dentists, journalists, and farmers who were pioneering the way in employment; on divorce, prostitution, women's history, the Church's role in the subordination of women, and even suggestions about nutrition and exercise. The paper also contained coverage on the topics and opinions George Train had desired in return for his financial participation. Each issue had space for his columns on subjects of his choosing (which he sent from jail) and for an informal financial column written by his friend David Melliss. Susan and Mrs. Stanton, not very interested in financial matters, paid little attention to the business column in their paper. They did not know how much hostility it was arousing in influential people such as financiers Jay Gould and Jim Fisk, who were able to keep advertisers away.

Former friends and colleagues continued to be angered by the editorial policy of *The Revolution* as well. They felt that by including so many wide areas of discussion, the paper

Susan B. Anthony's
feminist newspaper
The Revolution

The Revolution.

A TRUE REPUBLIC.—MEN, THEIR RIGHTS AND NOTHING MORE; WOMEN, THEIR RIGHTS AND NOTHING LESS

. V.—NO. 1.   NEW YORK, THURSDAY, JANUARY 6, 1870.   WHOLE NO. 105.

e Revolution.

LISHED WEEKLY, $2 A YEAR.

W YORK CITY SUBSCRIBERS, $3.20.

SINGLE COPIES, TEN CENTS.

ABETH CADY STANTON, Editor.

INA WRIGHT DAVIS, Cor. Editor.

N B. ANTHONY, Proprietor.

E, 49 EAST TWENTY-THIRD ST., N. Y.

Poetry.

NATURE.

NATURE, how fair is thy face,
light is thy heart, and how friendless thy
ce!
mistress of man! thou dost sport with him
atly
urs of ease and enjoyment; and brightly
smile to his smile; to his joys thou inclinest,
orrows, thou knowest them not, nor divinest.

wons, thou art wanton, thou lottest him love

art not his friend, for his grief cannot move

st, when he sickens and dies, what dost thou?
are thy garments, as careless thy brow,
laughest and toyest with every new-comer,
more for winter, a smile less for summer!
never an anguish to heave the heart under?
breast of thine, O thou feminine wonder!
one—the young, and the fair and the strong,
loved thee, and lived with thee gaily and
g,
now on thy bosom lie dead! and their deeds
days are forgotten! O hast thou no weeds
one year of mourning—one out of the many
s thy new bridals forever—nor any
or thy lost loves, concealed from the new,
idow of earth's generations? Go to!
and the night wind know aught of these
ngs,
not reveal it. We are not thy kings.

Be found in life that communion which links
woman but dreams, feels, conceives of and
nks
at man acts and is, concentrating the strength
nius within her affections at length
woman's full use through man's life, by man's
n
ed to forms fixed for life, the strong will
heart which the world's creeds now recklessly
aved,
a world's crimes the man of the world would
ro saved;
ed, as it were, the divine with the human,
ding the man, have completed the woman.

Extracts from "Lucile," by Owen Meredith.

ood, my dear, and let who will be biever,
noble things, not dream them all day long;
so make life, death, and the vast forever
ne grand sweet song.

CHARLES KINGSLEY.

[Entered according to Act of Congress, in the year 1869, by Alice Cary, in the Clerk's Office of the District Court of the United States, for the Southern District of New York.]

The Born Thrall.

BY ALICE CARY.

CHAPTER I.

THE BRICKMAKERS.

Hurr' up boys, hurr' up; its goin' to rain pitchforks; step to a double quick, and bring here the bricks that have been set into rows, and are dry 'nough to be sot into the kiln, and them 'taint dry 'nough, lay some boards onto. Hurr' up your cakes, I say!"

"Whew!" whistled a lad, who, having lost his boy's voice, and not yet gotten his man's beard, was not inclined to talk much; "Whew! whew!" He then unslipped the tow apron he was about tying on, threw it carelessly over the moulding-trough, and enquired of his nearest neighbor, what kept Mr. Killigrew away so long?

"What keeps him?" thundered the first speaker, "his own free will, I reckon; but no matter what keeps him, he isn't here and I am, and I am at the head o' the yard, and over you; so on with your tow apron agin, and at it with might and main, or I'll know the reason."

Walsh Hill, was the name of the man who fulminated this order, and having felicitated himself for a moment on the happiness of his rhetoric, he stepped forth from beneath the shed where the brick-kiln was beginning to take shape, wiped his muddy hands on his hair, and shook his fist at the youngest hand—the lad who had taken off his tow apron—in the very teeth of his command.

"Whew!" whistled the boy again, and then folding his arms, he leaned against the moulding-trough, as though, for his part, he saw nothing else to do.

Walsh Hill, feeling perhaps, that he could not enforce his order in that direction, turned to another of the hands—"What are you at, Mr. Go-easy?"—he said—"don't you hear, and don't you see it's a-goin' to rain like the devil, and all the bricks 'll be spilt?"

"My name's Barber, if I am the gentleman you're talking to," replied the man addressed as Mr. Go-easy, and then he added: "Seems to me your mighty considerate for other folk's interest, all at once—'taint five minutes past one yet, and Mr. Killigrew 'aint the man to waste much time—he'll be here himself directly and save all trouble."

"Mr. Barber," said Hill, coming forward and offering his hand, "I meant no disrespect to you, 'pon my honor as a gentleman, but I was throwed off my guard a little by this everlasting reference to Killigrew. I'm sick of his name, I hate it, and hate him into the bargain! No, no, sir; I wasn't putting on no airs, not to-wards you."

"I don't want you to *Mister* me," replied Barber, giving his hand. "A feller just talks to hear himself, sometimes, you know; but do think your hatred of Mr. Killigrew rather un-reasonable; come now!"

"I tell you, Mr. Barber"——

"Don't mister me, call me plain Joe, I don't want no handle onto my name."

"Well, then, I tell you, Joe, you don't know that rascal, he's bound for to keep ahead of us all, and for to keep us down."

"Don't b'lieve in that doctrine, one man don't keep another down if its into him for to go up—but it's going to rain, as you said, so let's to work." And thrashing his goad across the fly-bitten shoulders of the oxen, that stood with drooping faces and mired to their bellies in the pit, wherein they had been treading all the morning, he cried, "Come 'long, Buck! come 'long, Bright?" and, pulling their legs slowly out of the stiffened mortar, they began their weary round.

"Hold on!" exclaims Hill, "I want to bring you to your senses about this Killigrew—you're about half blind, but I think the scales would fall from your eyes, if I was to tell you a thing or two! Will you hear, or no?"

"Hain't the time to spare now—gee 'long, Buck!—gee 'long, Bright!"

Hill jerked the goad from the hand of his friend, and striking it across the honest faces of the oxen, brought them to a sudden halt. Poor beasts!—man had joined them together contrary to the wise intimations of nature. One had long legs, the other short; one had horns, of the longest and broadest, the other had no horns; one was lean, the other fat; one black and the other white. Even the rude man, who had struck them so wantonly, seemed to catch some faint perception of the unfitness of things, and to be moved with coarse compassion as he saw them standing there so mismatched, fetching short breath and lolling their tongues, for, lifting his hand, he sprang it like a trap against the quivering side of one of them, and then with his fingers combed away the loosened hair and murdered flies.

"In the first place," Hill began, "what business has old Killigrew to be away at this time o' day? its half an hour late."

"Not so much, and besides, he isn't the only one that's away. Mr. Smith isn't here."

"Well, sir!—Smith has got a right for to do perty much as he pleases! I hain't got a word to say agin Mr. Smith, he's got capital to back him—but old Sime Killigrew. Lord!"

"Its easy to say that, but I don't see that it means much."

"It means this much, Joe, it means that I hate him with the profoundest hatred—that's what!"

"No love lost, I reckon."

"Well, sir, I don't want none for to be lost onto my account, and you wouldn't nuther, if you knowed how he looks down onto you?"

"Looks down on me, does he! Well what do

was only hurting the women's cause. For some reason, it was Susan who was considered to be the bad influence on her co-editors. People were continually trying to win Parker Pillsbury and even Mrs. Stanton away from Susan's radical influence.

These negative reactions did not make it easy for Susan to start a subscription drive, but in her determined manner, she forged ahead. Congressmen were able to mail some items without cost, so Susan found a sympathetic Congressman who sent out ten thousand copies of the paper. She also went to Washington in an effort to persuade legislators to subscribe, which a number of them did. Some Congressmen who were opposed to Susan's viewpoints flatly told her they were subscribing in order to know what the other side was doing. She even waited in President Johnson's office for several hours and would not accept a refusal when he first declined to subscribe.

The Revolution not only reported the news, it managed to make some of its own. Now that Susan was working and living in New York City, she could see for herself the sad plight of working women. Their low wages, long hours, and dismal living and working conditions appalled her. The few labor unions that were active at the time were only open to men. The growth of industries was giving more and more women a chance to earn wages by working outside their home, but as far as Susan could see, they had just exchanged one form of bondage for another.

Susan had met a number of women from the newspaper trades in the course of trying to put out *The Revolution*. In the fall of 1868 she called a group of them together to discuss their mutual concerns. These typesetters, bookbinders, and clerks decided to form the Working Women's Association #1. Next, she got one hundred women from the sewing industries to join together as the Working Women's Association #2. Groups in other cities took her cue and soon news of various associations and their doings was being published in *The Revolution*.

Susan Anthony might have been the person who coined the phrase "equal pay for equal work," a rallying cry then and now for working women. Susan meant it, too. Upon hearing that some women objected to the heavy labor they had to do in the printing trades, she scolded them, saying that women in their homes had to put up with plenty of back-breaking work, and if they could not do what was expected of them, they had no business asking for equal wages.

Because of her observation of the mill workers and women who took jobs during the Civil War, Susan realized that women going into industry would acquire some independence from earning their own money. But she still felt it was important that they have the right to vote as well and urged the groups to fight for this. Her Working Women's Associations balked, however, at linking their cause to the suffrage movement. It was hard enough to organize around money and labor matters without aligning themselves with another unpopular cause. Susan disagreed, of course, and explained to the women that only when they could vote sympathetic legislators into office would their conditions be legally changed. She made some progress on the matter but she never really got the rank-and-file's support on this issue.

Along with suffrage, Susan was also passionate about raising funds for a training school that would cater to women who wanted to go into the printing trades. Her wish to have young working women in these professions soon got her into a great deal of trouble.

In 1869 the printers in New York went on strike. Susan visited some of their employers and told them it would be to their advantage to provide a training school that would turn out women to take the strikers' place. Susan obviously had not thought this idea through very well. Quite soon her innocently intended suggestion got back to the strikers. What she saw as a chance for women to get their feet in the door was seen by the National Typographical Union as a way to break the strike, and Susan was roundly criticized despite her explanations. When she tried to attend a national labor convention later that year, she was called an enemy of labor and denied admittance.

Susan was in trouble again when she and *The Revolution* brought the Hester Vaughn case to America's attention. Hester Vaughn was a poor working girl who was arrested for murdering her illegitimate child. The baby had been found dead beside her as she lay critically ill. Too poor to pay for a proper defense and tried before a prejudiced male jury, Hester was convicted even though there was no real evidence against her.

Susan and Mrs. Stanton maintained an editorial defense for her in *The Revolution*, and rival newspapers were outraged. They railed against *The Revolution* and its editors as immoral and accused them of advocating free love. Actually, *The Revolution* was trying to right the wrong done to the innocent Vaughn and at the same time point out that women lived under a different standard of morality from that of men. The case also gave Susan the chance to argue for the necessity for women jurors and women lawyers. Hester Vaughn was eventually pardoned, but Susan continued to receive scathing attacks for her defense of the girl long afterward.

About the same time, *The Revolution* took up arms on the "wrong" side of another notorious legal case involving a famous journalist, Albert Richardson, and his marriage to a divorced woman. The woman's estranged husband, named McFarland, shot Richardson for courting and marrying his former wife. Even though Mrs. Richardson had been divorced on the basis of McFarland's mental problems and brutality and had nothing to do with the shooting herself, the press portrayed her as a wicked woman who was somehow responsible for the tragedy. *The Revolution* rallied to Mrs. Richardson's cause, and when the court freed McFarland and also gave him custody of his child, Susan organized a protest rally that drew two thousand people.

The Revolution was published from January 1868 to May 1870. When George Train returned from England and realized how many people disliked his columns, he decided to pull out completely, hoping that this might raise circulation.

Susan wrote at the time: "Many people said they would subscribe if we dropped Train. We hope the fact that Train has dropped us will not invalidate these promises." It was too little and too late. The people who despised Train were not appeased.

When Susan's involvement with *The Revolution* ended, the paper was $10,000 in debt. It failed because it could not support itself. At its height, there were only three thousand subscribers, but there were many steadfast advertisers and Susan's family and friends had been remarkably generous with their loans and gifts. Susan had tried valiantly to keep the paper going. She had traveled and given speeches in hopes of gaining more readers and support. But with many of her potential subscribers and advertisers alienated, there was little chance of her ever being able to keep it going. Eventually, she had to give up control to two reformers who toned down the editorial content considerably, but they floundered and merged the paper with the uncontroversial *Christian Enquirer.*

The loss of her paper was a terrible blow to Susan. She said she felt as if she was signing her own death warrant. There was also the not insignificant matter of the $10,000 debt. Susan felt personally responsible for this. She could have easily declared bankruptcy as friends and family urged her to do, thereby cancelling her debt, but she refused. Her conscience and her feeling that defaulting would reflect badly on all women prevented her from taking the simple way out. Susan vowed that someday, somehow, she would pay off *The Revolution*'s debt.

THE FIRST WOMAN VOTER IN AMERICA

8

Just as *The Revolution* was a positive force in bringing all manner of issues to the attention of the public, it was also, in part, the cause of a major split in the women's movement.

The trouble that had been brewing because of the paper's content as well as the question of black versus woman suffrage came to a head at the American Equal Rights Association meeting in 1869. Susan and Mrs. Stanton attended the meeting and found themselves the object of an attack. One member of the association, Stephan S. Foster, rose and said the two women should not continue as officers of the Equal Rights Association because they were opposed to the Fifteenth Amendment, which would secure the black man's right to vote. Although the women won against the move to oust them, it was obvious that many members strongly resented the views presented in *The Revolution* as well as Susan and Mrs. Stanton personally.

Foster next attacked Susan on the grounds that she had misappropriated the association's funds and kept unreliable accounts. Henry Blackwell, Lucy's Stone's husband, was another of Susan's detractors, but as a member of the trust

An artist's interpretation of a meeting
of Susan B. Anthony's National Woman
Suffrage Association

fund committee he had recently checked the books and was able to vouch for Susan's accounts, if not her opinions.

With that harassment out of the way, the next issue on the floor was a motion supporting the Fifteenth Amendment. The Thirteenth Amendment had abolished slavery, the Fourteenth had established the citizenship of the blacks, but many people did not believe this amendment guaranteed their right to vote, so another amendment was needed. Frederick Douglass spoke eloquently for the motion, saying it was far more urgent for black men to get the vote than it was for women. Some of the women agreed, but Susan would not permit her beloved cause to be pushed to the background.

Her view was that if the convention could not support universal suffrage, they should at least rally around the concept of educated suffrage, making literacy a requirement for anyone who wanted to vote. This argument was never given much credence, and the association soon voted to support black male suffrage and the Fifteenth Amendment.

There were many mutterings by the ardent feminists in the group, and after the convention some of them got together at the Women's Bureau where the mutter grew into a vocal demand for a more women's-oriented equal-rights association. Out of the meeting was formed the National Woman Suffrage Association with Mrs. Stanton once again presiding and Susan on the executive board.

Now the split in the women's movement began to take on more shape and form. Susan's group, the "New Yorkers," consisted of Mrs. Stanton, Lucretia Mott, her sister Martha Wright, European free thinker Ernestine Rose, and many of the younger feminists who were eager to get the vote. Also in the New York camp were women from the Western states. Frontier women were not as sheltered as their Eastern counterparts and consequently did not shy away from issues such as marriage, divorce, birth control and labor reform. They had worked hard carving out the Western territory alongside men and they wanted their share of the rewards. This group liked the bold leadership of the Anthony-Stanton team.

On the other side of the fence was the "Boston" group, led by Lucy Stone and backed by such famous names as Lydia Mott and Amelia Bloomer. These women refused to be separated from the abolitionists and agreed that if only one moral victory for the vote could be won, it should be won by the black man.

Lucy Stone was outraged that Susan had formed a new women's group in which she, one of the movement's founders, had had no part. Also angry because women whom she considered radical had affixed the word "National" to their organization, Lucy decided to call her own convention to consider forming a rival group that would appeal to the more conservative segment of the movement.

Susan had been continuing with her usual schedule of lectures, conventions, and putting out *The Revolution* when she heard that Lucy was calling her own women's suffrage convention. Neither Susan nor Mrs. Stanton was invited.

Susan must have been hurt by this snub; she would have welcomed Lucy at her convention, she told friends. But rather than turn her back on the Boston group, she decided that even without an invitation she would attend the conference, which was to be held in Cleveland where Lucy Stone was now living. An old friend of Susan's, Judge Bradwell, was presiding over this meeting when Susan entered the hall. He asked her to sit on the platform with the other leaders, and in spite of some protests, she did take her place beside her adversaries.

The outcome of Lucy's convention was the formation of the American Woman Suffrage Association, a group that was far more sedate than Susan's "National." Susan spoke up for the need for a sixteenth amendment to the Constitution, but the Boston group decided they would work only for local state suffrage. Men were allowed to be officers of the American association, and the members also decided to keep strictly to the suffrage issue and not become embroiled in other controversial issues. Susan had hoped there could be some reconciliation between the two groups, but when she heard their aims, she realized that this would not be possible.

Yet she never dreamed the split would continue for twenty years, as it did.

One decision by the American Woman Suffrage Association affected Susan personally. As far as Lucy Stone was concerned, Susan's newspaper, *The Revolution*, had been tainted from the beginning. Now she and her group began to publish their more conservative views in their own newspaper, *The Woman's Journal*. A bland paper, it nonetheless had excellent financial backing and acquired a number of Susan's subscribers. *The Woman's Journal* was another nail in *The Revolution's* coffin.

Many people were unhappy about the rift in the women's movement and tried to bring the two sides together. This proved impossible, but as each group settled in, observers noted that though the American and the National women's suffrage associations were taking different routes, they were both working toward the goal of women's suffrage.

In 1872 some suffragists, as women who worked for the vote were called, as well as a few constitutional lawyers, decided that perhaps women already had that right. The first section of the Fourteenth Amendment states that all people born or naturalized in the United States are citizens and that states shall make no laws that would deny any person the rights of citizenship. The second section uses the word male but the first does not; nor does the Fifteenth Amendment, which states: "The right of citizens of the United States to vote shall not be denied . . . on account of race, color, or previous condition of servitude." The Fifteenth Amendment had been adopted in 1870.

The suffragists would have liked to see the words "or sex" placed in the Fifteenth Amendment, but since they were not, the women looked at the existing amendments with new interest. While the Constitution left it to the individual states to establish the qualifications for votes, it also stated that citizens or persons could not be denied the rights of citizenship. Were not women persons?

Between 1871 and 1872 more than one hundred women used this logic as a basis for attempting to vote. As early as

1868, women in Vineland, New Jersey, came to vote, but they were made to drop their ballots in separate ballot boxes, thus making it easy not to count them. Most of the women who tried to vote in the 1870s were stopped when they tried to register. A few did succeed in registering and voting, but again their votes were not counted.

Susan followed all these attempts at voting with a keen interest, and finally decided to test the law herself, turning to her sisters, Guelma, Hannah, and Mary for support. On November 1, 1872, the four of them walked into the barber shop where voter registration was taking place and said they wanted to register.

When the election judges told them this was not possible under New York law, Susan retorted that she was granted the privilege by the Fourteenth Amendment and proceeded to read them the pertinent section. This logic surprised the election judges, but after conferring, two of them finally agreed to register the Anthony sisters. An elated Susan then found fifty more women who also registered, though most of them backed out of voting in the actual election.

Four days later, on November 5, Susan voted in the general election. She was jubilant over her accomplishment, but at the same time, she realized that she might have broken the law. Unqualified people who voted in New York could be fined up to five hundred dollars. Voting inspectors who let this happen also faced legal action. Susan offered to pay the fines of the men who had registered her should it come to that, but there was not much she could do about the fact that if convicted they could receive up to three years in prison.

Newspapers buzzed about her bold move. As a sign that the times were changing and that the feminist message was finally getting through, some of the papers applauded Susan's action. The *New York Times* said it should earn her a place in history while the *Chicago Tribune* noted that she would make as good a candidate for public office as she would a voter.

Susan had consulted with her lawyer, Judge Henry R.

Selden, before she tried to register and he supported her interpretation of the Constitution. Her plan was this: after she successfully voted, she would bring suit against the many inspectors who had refused to register women or let them vote. If she won that suit, this would establish a legal precedent for women's suffrage. But Susan's plans never materialized because she was the one who was arrested.

On November 18, two weeks after she had voted, a deputy marshal came to Susan's house and informed her that she was under arrest. His warrant said that she had voted in an election violating a federal law stating that anyone who voted without having the legal right to do so was guilty of a crime.

This law had originally been passed to prevent Southern rebels from voting, and none of the legal advice Susan had received beforehand had hinted she might be tried under this stronger law. A startled Susan nevertheless rose to the occasion. When the embarrassed marshal who served her warrant suggested she might want to report to the United States Commissioner's office alone, she insisted he take her and even told him to handcuff her. He would not do that, but she finally made him accompany her on the trolley to the Commissioner's office. When the conductor asked for her fare, startled passengers heard her defiantly announce, "This gentleman is escorting me to jail. Ask him for my fare."

Susan's hearing was scheduled to take place a few weeks later, and she was arraigned on December 23; her bail was set at five hundred dollars. The other women who had voted were arraigned with Susan. If the spectators had expected to see a group of wild-eyed radicals they must have been disappointed. These lawbreakers were described by one newspaper as elderly women with thoughtful faces, the kind of matrons you might like to see taking charge of a sick room.

All of the women posted a five-hundred-dollar bail except Susan, who refused to do so. Her lawyer, Judge Selden, did not want his client put in jail so he paid it for her, a move that Susan quickly learned would prevent her case from being appealed to the Supreme Court because posting bail meant she was not challenging the lawfulness of her arrest. As Susan learned about this technicality, she rushed back to court, but it could not be undone. Selden's well-intentioned excuse that he could not permit a woman he respected to go to jail did not sit very well with Susan. But there was nothing else to do but begin planning for her trial.

During this ordeal Susan relied primarily upon Lydia Mott and stayed in her Albany home. From this base, Susan began to make speaking tours in the area and in Washington, D.C., where she handed out a summary of her argument to Congressmen. Her speeches at this time dealt specifically with what was happening to her. She wanted people to understand the legal points on which she based her right to vote and this she carefully explained in her speech, "The Equal Right of All Citizens to the Ballot." She told the story of her voting, her arrest and her upcoming trial in a speech entitled "Is It a Crime for A Citizen of the United States to Vote."

Susan was only free on bail and the United States Marshal was not very happy about her leaving town for speaking engagements, but she did not let that stop her. Many of these speeches were made in Monroe County where her trial was to be held. An alarmed district attorney thought so highly of her speaking abilities, he asked that the trial be moved to a different location because he felt she had prejudiced too many prospective jurors. The trial location was changed to Ontario County and Susan promptly began a speaking tour there.

Susan's trial began on June 17, 1873, in the tiny village of Canandaigua, New York. Her lawyers, her sister Hannah Mosher, and several other women friends accompanied her into the courtroom, which was packed with newspaper reporters, curious strangers, and some familiar faces, among them former President Millard Fillmore. Also sitting in the gallery was Judge Nathan Hall, who everyone had supposed would be presiding over the case. For undisclosed reasons he had turned it down.

Judge Hall had a reputation as being strict but fair. The judge Susan did face, Ward Hunt, had only recently been appointed to the bench and was considered unskilled. Moreover, his unfair treatment of Susan, which became evident throughout the trial, seems to have been politically motivated. His mentor and the man responsible for his judgeship was Roscoe Conkling, a United States senator from New York and a vocal opponent of women's rights.

Judge Hunt was a pale little man who sat on the bench in a shiny black broadcloth suit topped by a white cloth around his neck. Susan asked immediately if she could speak in her own defense. Judge Hunt quickly refused her request.

Her lawyer, Selden, maintained a masterful defense that pleased Susan. He told the court that Susan's only crime was that she was a woman. If she had been her own brother, everyone would have commended her for doing her civil duty by voting. Selden also explained that Susan honestly believed the Fourteenth and Fifteenth Amendments gave her the right to vote and consequently thought that in voting she was committing no crime.

Then it was the district attorney's turn. His argument was simple. No matter what Susan believed, the fact was she had broken the law. Judge Hunt agreed and in an unprecedented move, at the end of the summations, he took a written statement from his pocket and began reading. He told the jury that Susan was not given the right to vote by the Constitution and that her beliefs did not constitute a defense. "If I am right in this, the result must be a verdict . . . of guilty and I therefore direct that you find a verdict of guilty."

A furious Selden promptly rose to his feet and quite correctly told the judge that he had no right to give the jury that kind of instruction in a criminal case. The judge ignored him and told the clerk to record the verdict. When Selden asked that the jury be polled, Judge Hunt refused and dismissed the twelve jurors.

No matter what the newspapers thought about Susan and her cause, they were outraged by this miscarriage of justice. The *New York Sun* pointed out that Judge Hunt had impaneled the jury, and by not allowing them to be polled, he had violated Susan's right to a fair trial.

The next day, Henry Selden moved for a new trial arguing that Susan had been denied her right to a trial by jury. The judge denied the motion. Judge Hunt then made the mistake of asking the defendant if she had anything to say before she was sentenced. She certainly did.

Susan informed the court that her natural, civil, political and judicial rights had been trampled upon. At this point, Judge Hunt tried to stop her, but Susan plunged on. "I'm simply stating the reasons why sentence cannot be pronounced against me." The judge interrupted her again but Susan would not be thwarted. She told the judge that since she had not been given justice, nor even a fair trial, she demanded to have the fullest punishment the judge could mete out. Once more he ignored her and handed down her sentence—a fine of one hundred dollars.

"I shall never pay a dollar of your unjust penalty," she told the court. "All the stock in trade I possess is a $10,000 debt incurred by publishing my paper—*The Revolution*." She continued, telling the judge and the packed courtroom that unfair manmade laws taxed, imprisoned, fined, and hanged women while at the same time denying women representation in the government. She closed by saying she would continue to urge women to adhere to the maxim that "resistance to tyranny is obedience to God."

Judge Hunt was not impressed with this ringing speech. Then he made a clever legal move. He told Susan the court would not require her to be imprisoned until she paid her debt. If she had been put in jail, she might have been able to bring her case before the Supreme Court. Out of prison she could not, and so lost a second chance to have her case reviewed by the high court.

The day after the sentencing Susan attended the trial of the inspectors who had registered her. Their trial was almost a duplicate of Susan's, with the obnoxious Judge Hunt finding all the men guilty and then ordering the jury to implement that decision.

At least one juror objected to that order and tried to hold out until the judge's bullying finally coerced him into voting with the majority. Later, some of the jurors in both cases said that without Judge Hunt's instructions they would have voted not guilty.

The inspectors were charged twenty-five dollars each and court costs. Two of the inspectors refused to pay and were ordered to jail, where the women they had registered kept them supplied with excellent meals. Not long afterward, Susan asked some powerful political friends to intercede and the men received a pardon from President Grant.

Susan was very unhappy that her case had been reduced to the category of simple election fraud. She checked with many legal advisers, but they all agreed that because of the way the case had been structured and the wily legal manipulations, there was no way she could bring an appeal to a higher court.

Despite her keen disappointment, Susan turned her attention to a case that was going on in St. Louis. Virginia Minor, whose lawyer husband, Francis Minor, had been one of the first to suggest that women might have the right to vote under existing amendments, had herself brought suit against an inspector who had refused to register her. This case did reach the Supreme Court, but the Court ruled against Mrs. Minor, stating that the Constitution did not grant suffrage to anyone; that right was given to the states. All the Constitution could do was forbid discrimination on certain grounds through its amendments. Sex was not one of those grounds.

This decision by the Supreme Court was the final word on the subject. There was no way women could vote under existing federal laws. If women wanted the vote, they would have to continue the long struggle for a suffrage amendment of their own.

THE CONTINUING STRUGGLE

9

Susan was not personally able to win the vote for women through her court case, but public opinion was swinging toward the movement and to Susan herself.

The favorable reactions began to surface in 1870. To honor Susan's fiftieth birthday, and also the news that Wyoming and Utah territories had enfranchised their women citizens, some of Susan's friends gave a reception for her at the Women's Bureau in New York.

The newspapers duly noted this event and showered Susan with praise. The *New York Herald* hailed "Susan's Half-Century" while the *World* called her the "the Moses of her Sex." Susan must have been surprised to see such praise from former critics.

Later, after her voting trial, the *Rochester Express* described Susan as a refined warrior loved by all. As mentioned, many newspapers were furious that Susan had not received a fair trial and her dignity through this ordeal also won many to her side. Her detractors were still around, of course. Lucy Stone in *The Women's Journal*, editorially suggested Susan should have just waited until the laws were changed—"Then she can vote."

Once the trial was behind her, Susan had to turn her attention to urgent personal business. Her sister Guelma was very ill, and it was Susan's sad task to nurse her through her last days. After her sister's death, it was time for Susan to do something about the $10,000 debt she had assumed for *The Revolution*, as her creditors were becoming impatient.

Since the quickest way of making money was through public speaking, Susan signed up with the Lyceum lecture bureau and undertook another arduous trip through the Middle West and West. Many people, especially west of the Mississippi, were still not used to women speakers, and they came out in droves to hear the famous Susan B. Anthony. Many of them expected to see the sharp-tongued shrew they had heard about. Instead, they saw a proper, neatly dressed woman who won them over with her simple logic and friendly manner.

If the audiences were welcoming, the travel conditions were among the most difficult that Susan had ever encountered. She had always seemed to have the misfortune to travel during the worst weather, and this trip was no exception. Blizzards halted her trains, and travel to smaller towns was often done in open sleighs. Hotels were primitive and the food uniformly bad. While she traveled, her thoughts were with her sister Hannah and her mother, neither of whom were in good health, and with her sister Mary, who had to assume responsibility for the household while Susan was away earning money to reduce her debt.

Susan spoke on two topics at this time. The first was a stirring speech titled "Social Purity." If a woman speaker was still a novelty, one who spoke out about prostitution was almost scandalous. The point of Susan's speech was that men deserved a major share of blame for this problem. Poverty, along with a woman's lack of educational and employment opportunities, was often the reason a woman had to go into this way of life. Susan told her audiences that unless women had an equal chance to earn a living, these problems would escalate. Women also needed the vote so that they could help make laws relating to marriage, divorce, and rape, subjects that directly affected their lives. Susan also courageously spoke out about venereal disease, a taboo subject at the time. She expected to be attacked for her forthrightness. Instead, many newspapers praised her for the way she frankly dealt with a controversial topic.

Susan's other speech was titled "Bread and the Ballot." This topic won a good reception in the West, where people who favored rugged individualism were ready to listen to this message about women's suffrage. Men in the West appreciated that women had been a good influence on their untamed country, and they took the lead in getting their women the vote.

Though Susan's tour was arduous, she averaged only about $30 a day in fees. While in good weeks she could earn as much as $125, poor weeks might bring almost nothing. Still, she continued, always sending her sister Mary more money to put in the savings account for the debt repayment. Finally, through her own earnings, gifts from friends, and the savings of relatives, on May 1, 1876, Susan paid the last of her $10,000 debt—with interest. She said it was her day of jubilation.

Newspapers all over the country reported this event, calling it a moral victory. One said that she paid her debts like a man and then corrected itself, stating that not one man in a thousand would have paid the total amount.

With the burden of *The Revolution* lifted from her shoulders, Susan had the time to champion many women's causes. She continued her speaking engagements throughout the West and Middle West. She also continued to work for the passage of a sixteenth amendment that would insure women the right to vote, traveling to women's conferences all over the country. In addition, Susan began another pet project, the writing of a history of the women's movement.

By 1880 many of the first leaders of the movement, Martha Wright, Lydia Mott, and Lucretia Mott among them, had died. Susan and Mrs. Stanton, both in their sixties, were eager to start collecting the memoirs of the other trailblazers before it was too late.

Mrs. Stanton, like Susan, had been trudging around on the lecture circuit, and she was happy to stay home for a while to work on a book about the women's struggle. Susan moved in with her and after some initial problems finding a publisher, they began. Susan and Mrs. Stanton originally had in mind a one-volume book that would take a few months to finish. But as they started looking through clippings and letters, they realized this would be a far bigger project than they had envisioned. They called in another feminist, Matilda Joslyn Gage, to help, and the three sent out letters to people all over the country asking for their reminiscences. Most people were happy to comply, though they often did so by sending handwritten letters that were difficult to decipher. Lucy Stone responded with a curt note stating she never kept a diary and would not send a biography, and insisted the women not write one for her. Her hostility was not completely unexpected. Earlier, when her *Women's Journal* had published an honor roll bearing the names of the women who had worked for the cause, neither the name of Susan Anthony nor that of Elizabeth Cady Stanton was on it.

Mrs. Stanton did most of the actual writing on the history, while Susan, in her careful way, put together the material and checked the facts. She had saved almost every document from every convention, so there was much material to choose from. Matilda Gage wrote several chapters of the book and generally made herself useful to the two women.

The first volume of *A History of Woman Suffrage* was published in May of 1881 and Susan could not have been prouder of her own child. Many others were pleased with her effort too, and newspapers complimented the authors on their perception in seeing the need for such a work.

Using the profits from volume one, Susan and Mrs. Stanton financed volume two; this time gap until money started coming in left Susan with many unpaid bills. The steel engravings alone had cost a hundred dollars each, but Susan felt that pictures were as important as words in this book, so she commissioned them without concern about the cost. She also could have earned more money from the books if she had not given so many copies of them away—two thousand, by one estimate. Still, the women reasoned, it was necessary to get the books into schools and libraries, and if those institutions could not afford the expensive volume, Susan and Mrs. Stanton would see that they got it anyway. It looked as if Susan would once more be going into debt, but she received a letter from Wendell Phillips saying a wealthy feminist had recently died and left the bulk of her estate to be divided between Susan's group and Lucy Stone's. Not only was Susan thrilled with the amount—$25,000—but it also gratified her that despite their differences, Wendell Phillips had enough confidence in Susan to so graciously implement his client's wishes. This legacy helped finance the third volume of *A History of Woman Suffrage*, published in 1885, and took the story of the women's movement up to that time.

Susan breathed a sigh of relief when the history was completed. After the second volume was published, Mrs. Stanton went to England to visit her daughter, leaving Susan to do most of volume three. The work left her feeling restless; she was mired in the past, and as she told one young feminist, she preferred making history to writing it. Nevertheless, she was delighted that the facts and emotions of the women's struggle had been captured by two of its leaders, and for years afterward visitors would find her during a quiet moment happily thumbing through the books.

Susan could never stand to be away from Mrs. Stanton for too long; in 1883 she decided to take a vacation to Europe where she would not only see her friend but have the opportunity to talk to feminists in England and France as well. She became well acquainted with these leaders and returned to America with plans for the first International Conference of Women, which was eventually held in March of 1888 to commemorate the fortieth anniversary of the first women's rights convention. Fifty-three national organizations sent women. Delegates came from as far away as Norway, Finland, and India.

Back in the United States, after her visit to Mrs. Stanton, Susan was met by a new phenomenon. Temperance,

Susan's first cause, was fashionable again. The Woman's Christian Temperance Union, organized in 1874, was now headed by Frances Willard, an ardent feminist and suffragette. She was determined to link the cause of suffrage with temperance and argued that suffrage was needed, because with the vote, women could help outlaw drinking.

Many feminists were glad to have the WCTU members on their side. They were well organized, aggressive, and attracted many conservative women to the suffrage cause.

Susan, however, saw there were distinct disadvantages to this linkage, and as usual, she was right. The powerful liquor lobby quickly realized that women's suffrage meant votes for prohibition. By placing a small tax on liquor and spirits, they raised a great deal of money and spent it to fund lobbies and make contributions to the campaigns of legislators unfriendly to women's suffrage. Farmers, distributors, and saloon keepers were all expected to keep the women in their families away from reform movements, and those that did not were blackmailed and otherwise intimidated. The whiskey lobby with its money and influence was a Goliath compared to the meagerly funded Davids in the women's camps.

The beer and whiskey lobby also gained strength from the many immigrants who were pouring into America during the late nineteenth century. Many of these men not only liked liquor, they had a strong tradition of male superiority. They were not going to give up their drink or give women the vote.

Susan was just one of the many women angered by this situation. It was especially infuriating that foreign men, often illiterate and with no knowledge of history and perhaps no understanding of democracy, could use their vote to prevent American women from obtaining theirs.

Both the Republicans and Democrats courted the immigrant vote. Political bosses preyed upon the fact that these men did not really understand the system; often the immigrants sold their votes, sometimes figuratively in exchange for jobs or political favors, sometimes literally for money. Both parties knew that educated women voters would try to clean up these dirty political practices, so they worked with the liquor lobby to keep the vote out of the hands of women.

Susan very much admired the WCTU's Frances Willard, but on her speaking tours, Susan made it quite clear that she was asking for suffrage on its own merits, not to promote prohibition. Often she was asked to arbitrate between temperance and nontemperance members in the National Woman Suffrage Association. Despite her efforts to make the public understand the two causes were separate, they were indelibly linked in the minds of most voters and suffrage suffered because of it.

One good thing that did come out of the overlap was Susan's meeting with Anna Howard Shaw. Anna Shaw was one of the second generation of reformers who worked for the WCTU and who had also aligned herself with Lucy Stone and the American Woman Suffrage Association. Because of this affiliation, Susan expected not to like her, but she was surprised to find her a warm woman with an excellent speaking style, a quality Susan could never resist.

Howard, being a member of the American Association, naturally had heard some unflattering things about Susan Anthony and her group, but when she heard her speak at the International Council of Women, she quickly realized Susan was not the wild-eyed liberal she had heard stories about.

Many of the younger women who attended the International Council of Women felt the same way, and soon they began to talk about the two groups, forgiving their differences and joining together for the sake of their common cause. Neither the foreign delegates nor the younger members of either group really understood just what the split had been about anyway. In 1887 the membership of the American Association passed a motion directing their leader Lucy Stone to confer with Susan Anthony about the possibility of re-union.

There were plenty of old-timers who did remember the personal antagonisms, and the accusations flew back and forth for a while, but the younger women were so uninterested in these long-ago feuds that the leadership of both movements finally got down to serious discussions about how the groups could be merged. The question of who would be president seemed the major stumbling block. Lucy Stone thought that neither she, Susan, nor Mrs. Stanton should take that office, but there was a groundswell of support for Susan. Susan, however, used this support to throw the election to Mrs. Stanton, whom she modestly felt deserved it more than she did. So in 1890, Elizabeth Cady Stanton presided over the first meeting of the National American Woman Suffrage Association. Susan was the vice-president at large, while Lucy Stone took a place on the executive committee. The new organization had as its aims both state and federal suffrage amendments. With the rift healed, Susan was happy to start delegating some of her work to the younger women in the organization, or as she fondly called them, "her girls."

Now Susan turned her attention West. Many of the Western territories were beginning to enter the Union, and Susan was very hopeful they would come in as suffrage states. Congress, however, was making this difficult to do even when the states wanted it. Wyoming Territory had had women's suffrage for twenty years, but Democrats did not want any more Republicans coming in with this state than necessary, so they informed Wyoming that it would have to come in without women voters. The Wyoming legislature sent a telegram back stating they would stay out of the Union for a hundred years if their women could not vote, and the Democratic-controlled Congress relented.

This was only a small victory but Susan was determined to build upon it. Now seventy years old, Susan did not shirk from going with Anna Howard to the North and South Dakota territories, where they had to fight the liquor interests who were once more waging the battle against women's suffrage. This time it was summer rather than winter, but the journey was just as difficult. Public trasportation was generally unavailable, so the women rode in freight cars. The Dakotas, with their dry prairies, terrible heat, and hot winds, made the trip almost unbearable. All the hardships proved fruitless

Susan B. Anthony in her later years, surrounded
by photographs of her friends and mementos of the
women's movement to which she had devoted her life.

when, after six months of campaigning, women's suffrage was defeated in an election almost 2 to 1.

The grueling trip to the Dakotas convinced Susan that she should take a step she had been contemplating for some time. She wanted the younger women in the movement to assume the primary responsibility for organizing the West, while she would direct the many ongoing women's activities from her home in Rochester. Lucy Anthony had died in 1881, and now only Mary remained in the house. The two sisters decided that they would make splendid roommates and threw themselves into renovating and redecorating. It was with pride and relief that Susan set aside a corner for herself; she turned a room on the second floor into a study. In all her years of work Susan had never had her own desk. Now she spent many fulfilling hours there, writing letters, sending out memorandums and making plans while photographs of friends and family smiled down upon her from the desktop and walls.

There was a special reason that Susan was so happy to be settled in her house. She had hoped that Mrs. Stanton, now a widow, would come and stay with her for a protracted length of time. She was eager to have her old friend settle down to some serious writing.

But Mrs. Stanton had different ideas. She insisted upon living in New York and working on a special writing project she had in mind. Susan wanted her to devote herself to the suffrage issue, but Mrs. Stanton, always of a more philosophical bent, had decided to tackle nothing less than rewriting the Bible. Mrs. Stanton was still firm in her belief that the Church was one of the main causes of the subordination of women. She wanted to write *The Woman's Bible*, a new translation and reinterpretation. She was sure that with a proper translation, she could prove that inferiority of women was not the Bible's intent.

Susan agreed with this idea in principle. But she feared that writing *The Woman's Bible* would open a can of worms that would not only provoke the fire-and-brimstone accusations against the feminists but would also divert Mrs. Stanton's energies from more practical issues.

This disagreement caused major problems between the two old friends. When *The Woman's Bible* was finally published in 1895, it caused just the uproar Susan had foreseen. Suffragettes were attacked and tried futilely to explain that Mrs. Stanton's views were her own. Worse, many of the young feminists totally disagreed with the idea of *The Woman's Bible*, and while Susan did so in private, these religious conservatives staged an open rebellion at the women's convention in 1896. Many of the young women Susan considered "her girls" not only disavowed *The Woman's Bible*, they wanted a resolution passed condemning it. Susan was terribly upset by this. She and Mrs. Stanton might have had disagreements on the subject, but a public attack on the book was an attack on her dearest friend.

Susan was chairing the women's convention, and she stepped down from the podium to express herself on the motion. She spoke harshly, accusing the convention of showing intolerance. "When this platform is too narrow for all to stand on, I shall not be on it." She told the women how fifty years before, Lucretia Mott had thought Mrs. Stanton would injure the women's cause by insisting that suffrage be placed in the original list of demands. Time had proven Mrs. Stanton correct. Now the convention wanted to pass a resolution that would be a vote of censure upon a woman "without peer in intellectual and statesmanlike ability."

Despite Susan's rhetoric, the resolution condemning *The Woman's Bible* passed. She was so dismayed that the members had ignored her moving speech and sincere sentiments, she was tempted to resign, as was Mrs. Stanton. Finally, they both decided they could do more within the organization than from outside it, but in private Susan did rebuke her girls and told them they were setting up an inquisition.

With Mrs. Stanton spending much of her time visiting her daughter in England and after the death of Lucy Stone,

Susan was the last of the old guard actively involved in women's rights. Aunt Susan, as she was affectionately called, was now seventy-two years old but kept up the active pace of a woman half her age. She went everywhere and did everything. She talked about her cause with all sorts of people, from Wild West showman Buffalo Bill to President Grover Cleveland. She guided the National American Suffrage Association, dominating the annual conventions. And when she took time out from her travels and talks, she worked on her memoirs with her biographer, Ida Husted Harper. Susan had met her in Terra Haute, Indiana, where Mrs. Harper was the only feminist in the town.

In spite of the growth and the continuing acceptance of the movement, Susan was still unhappy about how relatively few women participated in the women's movement. On the other hand, she was well aware of the strides that had been made. She wrote to Mrs. Stanton near the end of that woman's life: "We little dreamed that when we began . . . fifty years later we'd be compelled to leave this battle to another generation of women. But . . . they enter upon this task equipped with college educations, with business experience, with the freely admitted right to speak in public."

A few weeks later Mrs. Stanton died and Susan hardly knew how to contain her grief. She told the newspaper reporters that if she had been the one to die, Mrs. Stanton would have known how to describe their friendship in beautiful phrases, but she was not able to put into words all that they had meant to each other.

Recuperating from the loss of her friend must have been incredibly difficult for Susan. This was the last in a long list of losses. She had outlived most of her friends. Her brother Merritt had died unexpectedly, and then her brother Daniel passed away. Out of the large Anthony family, only she and Mary remained. But Susan continued going to conventions and to Europe for international meetings, a quick, bright-eyed woman easily noticed in a crowd because of her clothes which were now her trademark—a black silk dress and a red shawl. She remained the essence of plain speaking and common sense, her courage, enthusiasm and vision of the future never wavering. During the last six years of her life Susan suffered from a heart condition, but this did not stop her.

One of her last public appearances was at a women's convention in Baltimore. A speaker that night said that to Susan Anthony belonged, more than to any other woman in the history of the world, the love and gratitude of all women in every country. A few weeks later, at her eighty-sixth birthday celebration, she had her own words of praise to speak. She told her guests that with so many true and dedicated women devoting their lives to the cause, "Failure is impossible." Less than a month later, in 1906, she died at her home in Rochester.

Susan did not live to see women get the vote—that was not to happen for another fourteen years. In 1920 the Nineteenth Amendment to the Constitution was ratified, its form exactly the same as when it was first introduced in Congress forty-two years earlier. The amendment's language was simple but powerful. It stated that "the right of citizens of the United States to vote shall not be denied or abridged by the United States or any state on account of sex." At long last women were entitled to all the rights and privileges guaranteed to citizens. During the final days of the women's suffrage campaign, workers popularized the amendment by calling it the Susan B. Anthony Amendment. They did this partly to honor the woman who had done so much to make this dream a reality and also because they knew the popularity Susan had enjoyed would help their cause in a practical way.

Passage of the amendment was an important achievement but it was not the end of the women's struggle. In many ways it was just the beginning. American women continued to fight for equal educational opportunities, the right to enter careers previously considered to be for males only, and to be paid the same wages as men. In their personal lives it was not until the 1970s that women in great numbers took for themselves the option to be married or stay single, and to have children or not. All of these advances are still viewed with suspicion by some segments of society.

After Anthony's death, women continued
to demonstrate for the right to vote until
the 19th amendment to the Constitution
was finally ratified in 1920.

By any standard, it is clear that women have a much stronger place in American society than they did 150 years ago. Even Susan Anthony lived long enough to see the unalterable changes in the fabric of the country. At the last national women's convention she attended in 1906, Susan could look around and see college-educated women and those pursuing careers in everything from medicine to social work. There were women at the conference from four states that had already granted suffrage to women—Wyoming, Colorado, Utah, and Idaho. Fifty years before, women were reviled if they dared speak in public. Now the women's movement had produced a whole generation of speakers who would continue to raise their voices in the cause for women's rights. None of this could have been achieved without the bold women who fought the long, bitterly contested fight to be treated like rational human beings. At the forefront among these women was Susan B. Anthony.

Susan defied convention, stood up for what she believed was right, and dedicated herself to equality for all people no matter what their sex or color. When she started her lonely battle she was held in contempt by the general public, but by the time she died Susan was a beloved national figure. She accomplished this by the force of her own personality and the righteousness of her cause. The United States government honored her seventy years after her death by putting her image on a new coin, the Susan B. Anthony dollar. American women for generations to come will revere her as one of the country's founding mothers.

FOR FURTHER READING

Anthony, Katharine. *Susan B. Anthony: Her Personal History and Her Era.* New York: Doubleday, 1954

*Coolidge, Olivia. *Women's Rights.* New York: E. P. Dutton, 1966

*Faber, Doris. *Petticoat Politics.* New York: Lothrop, 1967

Gurko, Miriam. *The Ladies of Seneca Falls.* New York: Macmillan, 1974

Harper, Ida Husted. *The Life and Work of Susan B. Anthony* (3 vols). New York: Arno, 1969

Hymowitz, Carol and Michaele Weissman. *A History of Women in America.* New York: Bantam, 1978

Lutz, Alma. *Susan B. Anthony.* Boston: Beacon Press, 1959

Stanton, Elizabeth Cady. *Eighty Years and More Reminiscences 1815–1897.* New York: Schockon Books, 1971.

*Denotes books of interest to younger readers.

INDEX

Red Cross, 62
Revolution, The, 77, 78–80, 82, 85, 89, 98, 99
Richardson, Albert, 82
Rose, Ernestine, 87
Rousseau, Jean Jacques, 11–12
Rush, Benjamin, 24

St. Louis Suffrage Assoc., 74
Scott, Dred, 58
Selden, Henry, 90–91, 93, 94
Seminary for Females, 13–14
Shaw, Anna Howard, 103
Slacks for Women, 49, 50. *See also* Bloomer costume
Slavery, 26–27, 57–59. *See also* Abolitionists
Smith, Gerrit, 30, 35
Society of Friends, 9
Sons of Temperance, 25, 40
Stanton, Elizabeth Cady, 21, 22, 28, 29–30, 31, 32–35, 37, 40, 41, 42–43, 44, 46–47, 48, 50–52, 56, 64, 68, 69
Stanton, Henry, 32, 65, 87, 100, 106
Stone, Lucy, 28, 37–38, 39, 40, 42, 52, 53–54, 55, 97, 104
Suffrage
    black, 66, 69
    women's, 66–67, 69, 74, 81, 90–91, 97, 106, 109
Suffragists, 89
Sumner, Senator, 66, 67
Susan B. Anthony Amendment, 109

Temperance movement, 20, 24–25, 102
Textile mills, 6
Thompson, George, 32
Thirteenth Amendment, 64, 66
Train, George Francis, 74–78, 82
Training school, 81
Trousers for women, 50
Troy Female Academy, 13
Truth, Sojourner, 69

Uncle Tom's Cabin, 57
Underground Railway, 27, 57, 58

Vaughn, Hester, 82
Voting privilege for immigrants, 102

Willard, Emma, 13
Willard, Frances, 102, 103
The Woman's Bible, 106–107
Women's Bureau, 87, 97
Women's Christian Temperance Union (WCTU), 103
Woman's Journal, The, 89, 97, 100
Women's Loyal League, 66
Women's movement
    official beginning of, 23
    organization of, 2
    split in, 85, 87
Women's National Loyal League, 64
Women's rights convention, 21, 23, 42, 67
Women's State Temperance Society, 41, 42, 43
Working Women's Assoc., 80, 81
Wright, Martha, 87

ABOUT THE AUTHOR

Ilene Cooper is a graduate of the University of Missouri, where she majored in journalism before going on to earn a master's degree in library science at Rosary College. She has written for television and magazines and currently serves as a consultant for ABC Television's "After School Specials." Ms. Cooper lives in Chicago, where she works as a book reviewer.

B

8.42   copy 1

ANTH   Cooper, Ilene
        Susan B. Anthony